A Call to Manhood: In a Fatherless Society

by **David E. Long**

HUNTINGTON HOUSE PUBLISHERS

Huntington House Publishers
P.O. Box 53788
Lafayette, Louisiana 70505

Library of Congress Card Catalog Number 93-78464
ISBN 1-56384-047-2

Printed in Bogota, Colombia

Dedication

To my earthly father, William George Long, Jr.,
who laid the foundation in my life;
To my father in the faith, Pastor William David Young,
who helped me build upon that foundation;
and
To my heavenly Father,
Who called me into His glorious presence.

Contents

═══════════════════════════════════

───────── **PART III** ─────────
Turning the Hearts
═══════════════════════════════════

Acknowledgments

Special thanks are due my faithful and brilliant wife, Diana, who was the initial voice that encouraged me to write the book you now hold in your hands and whose patience and servant heart made it possible to meet our deadlines;

my children, Jennifer, Angela, Jeremiah (and the yet unnamed one still in the hopper), who showed great patience and understanding during the intense months of writing;

my good friend, Randall Terry (I knew him when he was still "Randy."), whose enthusiasm, insight, and obnoxious optimism pushed me over the edge in making the decision to write;

Mike Bagwell, Mary Dain, Scott Dawson, Jerry Tallo, and David Young, whose editorial assistance and input was a tremendous help in fine-tuning the language and sharpening the message;

Mark Brown, Mary Lou Mikel, and Jeanine Richardson, who assisted me in the research;

Kristen Renz and Francine Helligam, whose help in the final stages and review process kept us on course;

the many men whose stories have enriched my understanding and taught me perhaps more about the struggles of modern manhood than I could have learned any other way;

Peter Monacelli, Jim Moore, and Dennis Peacocke, who loved me enough to invest themselves as "uncles" and mentors in the process of fleshing out this message;

Bob, Dan, Doug, Jeff, John, Mark, and Steve, for courageously and patiently exploring the Journey to Manhood with me;

and, my editor, Mark Anthony, and the outstanding team at Huntington House, whose encouragement and Kingdom skill have made this book possible.

Introduction

The day had been long . . . meetings with staff . . . reviewing notes for a news conference . . . preparations for an upcoming radio show . . . finishing touches on an article for a national publication . . . a batch of phone calls . . . last minute arrangements for a quick trip to Wichita . . . a newsletter deadline.

It'd been another day in the life of a small-town, pro-life organization.

Climbing into bed, I reached for something to read while I waited for my wife. I was contemplating inviting Dr. Anthony Evans, president of the Urban Alternative, to be our guest speaker at an upcoming pro-life banquet; and I had picked up his recent book, *America's Only Hope*, to see what the man had to say about changing the culture. After setting the slip cover aside and glancing briefly at the table of contents, I leafed forward to page 11. And then I saw it, his prologue to chapter 1—the fateful nursery rhyme:

Humpty Dumpty sat on a wall.
Humpty Dumpty had a great fall.
All the king's horses,

And all the king's men,
Couldn't put Humpty together again.

Life changing, isn't it? Well, it was for me.

For nearly a year, I had been studying the crisis in American manhood and was developing new teaching material for men along the lines of what I was referring to as the principles of "Kingdom Manhood." Dr. Evans' use of the Humpty Dumpty metaphor helped put things into focus for me.

You see, in Dr. Evans' apologue, Mr. Dumpty symbolizes our modern Western society, and the "king's men" are the guys in Washington, D.C., who are attempting to put Humpty back together again. Because of our culture's orientation toward secular humanism, many Americans have progressively elevated the government, and particularly the president, to the place of "king." That is to say, most have begun to look to the institution and people of government as our nation's lord and savior.

Though the nice people on Pennsylvania Avenue may be sincere, I think it is becoming increasingly obvious that civil government will never put Humpty back together again. In fact, the way they positioned him on the wall was precarious and unbalanced to begin with. Whether they knew it or not, they set him up to fall—it was inevitable.

In reality, Mr. Dumpty does not need to be rebuilt; he needs to be *reborn*. Even if we could "fix" him, which we cannot, were we to put him back up on the wall, he would eventually fall off again.

Over two hundred years ago, a professor by the name of Alexander Tytler suggested that societies built squarely upon the unrestrained democratic will of the people are destined to run their course in about two hundred years. Thus he says:

> A democracy cannot exist as a permanent form of government. It can only exist until the voters discover that they can vote themselves largesse from the public treasury. From that moment on, the majority always votes for the candidates promising the most benefits from the public treasury, with the result that a democracy always collapses over loose fiscal policy, always followed by a dictatorship.

The average age of the world's greatest civilizations has

been two hundred years. These nations have progressed through this sequence: From bondage to spiritual faith; from spiritual faith to great courage; from courage to liberty; from liberty to abundance; from abundance to complacency; from complacency to apathy; from apathy to dependence; from dependence back again into bondage.[1]

Has the clock simply run out on this experiment we call Western culture. Perhaps Humpty is on the ground in a million pieces. Perhaps the idol is broken, and it cannot be repaired.

Nevertheless, all is not lost, for the true "King's men" are not the ones found in the halls of Congress; they are the ones found in the church, and they have yet to emerge on the scene. When they do, things will look very different.

*   *   *   *   *

This is a book about the unfolding cultural crisis in America. From the angry Feminist movement to the anti-war pacifists, from the Oval Office to the television and radio talk-show circuit, from the pastoral study to the Federal Reserve Board, from the arts community to the world of commerce, from nearly every sector of society, people are beginning to admit the obvious—Mr. Dumpty has fallen off the wall. Most would also readily admit that the men who are trying to put him back together again are failing at the task.

The progressive collapse of Western culture is fundamentally a collapse in American leadership on every level. Moreover, because men have been appointed by God to provide servant leadership to the three primary spheres of society—the church, the state, and the family—and because, whether we like it or not, men are still the predominant leaders in these three realms, the crisis we face is ultimately the manifestation of a crisis in American manhood. Therefore, this is a book about men.

But it is not about all men. It is about men who are increasingly aware of an inner longing to find and serve the true King. It is about men who yearn to discover and walk in a genuine definition of virility. It is about men who are tired of living in the disappointing illusion of the so-called "American Dream." It is about men who have become desperate enough to want to discover their true purpose and destiny. It is, therefore, about men destined to change the course of a nation. It is about the true King's men.

If you are a man seeking for truth, this book is about you. May you find the King.

Part I

Where Are All
the King's Men?

1.

Man of the Year

*For the anxious longing of the creation waits eagerly for the
revealing of the sons of God.*

Romans 8:19

Standing at the counter, waiting for my insurance agent to
return with my paperwork, I noticed a recent edition of *Time*
magazine sitting on the coffee table in the lobby. The bold
headline leaped at me from across the room with these words,
"MAN OF THE YEAR." And below the heading was the name
Ted Turner (the founder and owner of Cable News Network).

Later, after reading through the article, I was shocked by
what I found. Although astonishingly successful in the business world, Mr. Turner's personal life read like a tragic novel.

Marital unfaithfulness, multiple divorces, alcoholism, fits of rage and violence (mostly verbal, but sometimes physical), bouts with manic-depression, talk of suicide, and the fear of assassination were all displayed for the world to see. Psychiatric counseling and lithium finally helped "tame" the rage in Ted's soul at about age fifty.

As I stood there reflecting on the pitiful saga of Mr. Turner's life, our national "MAN OF THE YEAR," I mused to myself, "Unbelievable! Unbelievable! Whom are they trying to kid?"

I began to realize that every society has its male icons, men bigger-than-life to those who are small in their own eyes. These are the men that we claim to have found in our desperate search for manhood. They embody real "manliness" according to the standards set by popular culture.

It also became apparent to me that the *Time* cover story reflects our society's active search for these male icons, a real and dynamic undercurrent in modern culture. There seems to be an emotional need for people to discover male heroes, men we common folk can look up to. Furthermore, if real heroes are in short supply, society is often all too willing to enthrone small men in their stead. Unwittingly, we are highly committed to a historical and biblical idea—we need "real men" in our land.

Obviously, Ted Turner is one of our cultural icons, but is he a "real man"?

In Search of a Real Man

The search for genuine manhood in America is gaining fresh momentum as we near the end of the twentieth century. Innately, we all seem to know that we need real men. Occasionally, Hollywood claims to have found some. The marines are still looking. Millions of American voters watch the various political races each year in hopes of finding one or two that they can endorse, or at least tolerate, come November. We all know of countless unmarried women who are involved in the search, some desperately so. Fathers and mothers eagerly seek them among their children. At the same time, millions of fatherless boys and girls are longing for one to call dad. Everywhere we look people are anxiously seeking to find the real men.

Even forces in the unseen world have engaged in the search. The Bible tells us that Satan roams the earth, looking about for some men (see Job 1:7). His demonic lust is to find those whom he can devour (see 1 Pet. 5:8.). God is also traveling the face of the globe in a divine quest to find some "Kingdom" men willing to join Him in His destiny of destroying the works of the devil (1 John 3:8).

In the natural and in the spiritual, on the earth and in the heavenlies, the search is on.

The Measure of a Modern Man

What is it about Mr. Turner that the editors of *Time* would bestow upon him the venerable title of *"Man* of the Year"? Is this simply the liberal media's propaganda? Or have we actually adopted a new standard for manhood in America?

In modern Western society, apparently three primary traits seem to have emerged as the test of true virility. Find these, popular culture says, and you have found a real man. They are (1) a measure of natural talent, (2) an appearance of vocational success, and (3) raw ambition. Think about it. Consider some of your favorite male movie stars, sports characters, or music artists, or those men whom you hold up in the business or political world as special. Do these three qualities appear? In most cases the answer is probably *yes!*

And why not? There is nothing intrinsically evil about natural talent, vocational success, or raw ambition. It is interesting to note, nevertheless, that as these traits are detected, numerous character flaws may often be overlooked: for example, unfaithfulness, as in the case above with Mr. Turner. Virtue and integrity are not necessarily essential. Honesty and a demonstrable sense of true righteousness may be conspicuously absent. That which is on the "inside" of a man is overlooked for that which is visible. Like the ancient prophet Samuel, we have become preoccupied with the superficial stature of a man in our search for one we can elevate to "king" (1 Sam. 16:6, 7).

Understanding this exterior and shallow three-point measuring rod, we can easily see why society puts forth the male heroes that it does. We can also glimpse the reason why real men are in short supply throughout society.

Where Are All the Real Men?

Beyond the pages of *Time* magazine, we must press further into society to see whether or not we will find some real men. Surely somewhere in the male-dominated realms of our culture, we will locate the missing pool of genuine masculinity.

In our search I would like to focus on three key institutions where men have traditionally dominated and demonstrated leadership in American history—the state, the Church, and the family. If we can find some real men here, we will likely find them scattered throughout the rest of society as well. Of course, the converse is also true; if the pool of virility runs low in these three primary spheres, we can be certain that our culture is in trouble.

Shortage in the State House

Politics in America is undergoing tremendous turmoil as more and more male civil officials are discovered to be thieves, adulterers, incompetents, and bribe-takers. Nonetheless, most of our public leaders, especially on the federal level, do embody the tri-fold real man criteria of our popular culture. Consider their significant talent (ability to obtain votes and give impressive speeches), their incredible vocational achievements (they got elected before), and their outstanding ambition (they work very hard at all of this), and you can see that they, in fact, do pass this accepted test of modern manhood.

But we also find that among these same characters greed, sexual perversion, financial ineptitude, thievery, pride, and dishonest gain are just as prevalent. For example, the 1992 House banking scandal revealed that over three hundred of our congressional leaders had been having difficulty in balancing their checkbooks. Overdrafts totaled more than 10 million dollars between 1989 and 1990 alone. A few had overdrawn their accounts as many as eight hundred times during their term in office.

The reality that the standard of virility for political leadership was indeed adjusting to this new three-point test was driven home to me during the 1992 presidential elections. Having just begun work on this book, I was interested in the campaign from the perspective of the moral character of the three main candidates. I watched the Gennifer Flowers sex scandal rumors blow in like a thunderstorm and blow over just as quickly. Most incredibly, the American public seemed to lack any serious interest in the alleged twelve-year affair that Flowers claimed she had with Clinton. There was no national outcry for an investigation. Unlike the newsstand tabloids, the major media did their best to ignore the allegations and the implications.

The issue is not Mr. Clinton's innocence or guilt; the issue is the public's lack of interest in the moral character of a national leader. Presented with an opportunity to look "inside" the man, to see the heart, we chose rather to focus on the exterior. After all, the stature was incredible—surely this must be our king.

Similarly, most politicians these days are not measured by standards having to do with personal ethics, family fidelity, sexual purity, or honesty. Rather, society now measures their public persona—the show!

Are these male politicians real men?

The Hunger for a Real Husband

Like our civil servants, many husbands are also not faring well in these troubled times.

Some women who married their husbands because of talent (they put on an impressive show and talked a "good talk"), apparent career success (he has a good job), and raw ambition (tenacity during the chase), are now, after tying the knot, becoming disillusioned with the man of their dreams and wish they had awakened before the wedding day.

Though it is hard to believe, several recent surveys reflect that about half of the married men in America will commit adultery sometime during their marriage.[1] Incredible as this may seem, the problem of marital unfaithfulness is actually larger than these figures demonstrate. Speaking at men's gatherings and leading men in personal and corporate repentance on many occasions, I have observed that the incidence of "adultery of the heart" (Matt. 5:27, 28) is much higher than any formal study could show. For every man who actually commits adultery, many more have considered or engaged in it in their hearts. In fact, an oft-cited study of college students showed that a majority of the male sophomores polled would rape a woman if they knew they would never get caught.[2] This incredible "I-would-if-I-could", relativistic mindset carries over a few years later into the marriages these men will make.

Many more husbands are too aggressive and even abusive with their wives. The FBI estimates that between 4 and 6 million woman are abused in their homes each year.[3] Though the data reflects a disturbing upward trend, it is again probably under-reporting the immensity of the real situation. Many abused women are reluctant to turn in their husbands for fear of physical reprisal or because they want to protect their husbands from the consequences of their abusive actions.

Aggression has an equally vile counterpart—the passive husband. This type of man is not necessarily doing anything wrong; rather, he seems to be immobilized—incapable of doing anything right. He demonstrates, by his lack of initiative and energy, an unwillingness to lead either in practical family affairs or spiritual matters. He is in neutral.

Many women also complain of not feeling loved by their husbands. Though this sense of rejection is hard to define and therefore difficult to track statistically, the increasing rate of family splits is perhaps the most solid indication of this phenomenon. Women are leaving their men in record numbers, with 60 percent of all first-time marriages now ending in divorce,[4] and researchers say the upward trend will probably increase as we near the year 2000.[5] "No-fault" divorce laws notwithstanding, a woman who truly feels loved is not about to take advantage of the law or the independent atmosphere of the day and throw her husband out. I wonder how many women when filing for divorce have listed as the cause: "I was loved too much by my husband." Skyrocketing divorce rates are not about freedom, feminism, or independence; they are about women not feeling loved by their husbands. This sense of rejection may also explain why nearly as many women as men are pursuing extramarital affairs during their mid-life years.[6]

The failure of America's husbands is fast approaching epidemic proportions. From the unloving to the unfaithful, from the emotionally passive to the physically aggressive, husbands are failing to keep their wives happy.

The Dad Deficit

The other role we must look at in measuring the success of men in the family is that of fathering, where we find a similar breakdown occurring.

For instance, although fathers are traditionally expected to protect their children from the harms of the adult world, parental child abuse continues to increase with fathers being the primary abusers. Recent research indicates that as many as 25 percent of all children in this country will experience some form of sexual abuse before age seventeen and that girls are four times more likely to be abused than boys.[7] Incredibly, this means that one out of every five girls will be sexually abused before her seventeenth birthday, probably by her own father or another male authority figure.

In addition to sexual abuse, many children suffer physical violence, with more than one million children "severely abused" each year in the home.[8]

More and more dads are having trouble keeping their families together, many outright abandoning their children. Some 12 million children, or almost one in five, are being raised by single moms.[9] Twenty-six percent of all children born in 1991 were born to unmarried women.[10] In 1989 nearly 80 percent of single family homes were headed by women.[11]

When families break up, men often "give" the children to the wife and, in many cases, shirk their responsibility to their offspring by withholding support and spending little time with their kids. Some 12.7 million children in America live in poverty, and more of these reside with a female (maternal) head of household than all other housing situations combined (such as grandparents, the father, or a sibling).[12] Even fathers who are at home are often "emotionally absent" or simply too consumed with their own careers or hobbies to provide good fathering to their children.

The emerging picture of the American family is one of deepening devastation and destruction. Moreover, the impending implosion in the home is unquestionably related to the weakening ability of men to fill their roles as effective husbands and fathers. Issues of root cause and blame aside, we can no longer ignore the tragic indicators that the American father/husband figure has seen better days.

Are these fathers and husbands real men?

The Male Crisis in Christendom

Searching society for real men has, throughout history, led many to the Christian Church. Here we would think we might find real men of godly stature, real men of holy faith, real men of moral integrity. After all, our heritage is that of martyrs, saints, and radical reformers. Our Christian history books tell of men recounted as the courageous, the noble, and the committed. If there are real men to be found anywhere, surely it must be in the ranks of the modern-day Christian Church.

Unfortunately, this is not the case.

The body of Christ has placed the same misguided emphasis on the three outward measures of manhood as has society at large. Sadly, like most of the men of the culture, many men in the Christian Church also believe that what really matters is that we demonstrate some external talent, vocational achievement, and a lot of ambition. In church after church, city after city, I have seen these attributes elevated as supreme ideals.

Consider some of the nationally recognized Christian men whom we have idolized during the eighties—men who were obviously talented, undeniably successful, and terribly ambitious. We have revered these as great men of God, and certainly some of them have done much good. But the tragic reality is that many men who were once held up as great Christian leaders are now among the fallen.

They were so talented! They were so successful! They were so ambitious! They were our Christian "men of the year"! But were these Christian leaders real men?

I am convinced that the fallout and exposure of our Christian superstars is just the tip of the iceberg. If the moral underpinnings are weak among the clergy and leadership, how much more so among the "pew people"? But the failure of manhood in the church must be considered on another level. What has been our stand of righteousness in a day of growing evil? Have we realized the high call of being a "city set on a hill," a bright light of moral courage, a place of towering integrity? Or has the bumper sticker that reads, "Christians aren't perfect, just forgiven," become our scapegoat for righteousness—our new crutch and creed?

Have the men of the church taken to the streets in moral outrage over the savage murder of every third baby conceived? Have we become incensed enough over the horrific atrocities of child pornography to set aside our pursuits of personal comfort and safety and fight for the children? Have we taken the widow and the orphan into our homes to visit them in their affliction (James 1:27), or have we sent them, by default, into the welcoming arms of Planned Parenthood and Social Services? Have the men of the church willingly sacrificed their time and money—maybe even their reputation—to stand against the swelling tide of cultural evil?

Can the secular community look to the men of the church as standard bearers, as pillars of truth and righteousness, and as bright lights in a day of intense darkness?

By and large, it appears that Christian men have lost the will to stand for righteousness. Our actions fail to match our words—the high ideals of our hymns and creeds. Because the church is led by these weak-willed men, Christianity in America has succumbed to corporate passivity and accommodation with societal evil.

The late Dr. Francis Schaeffer spoke of our moral frailty:

> Here is the great evangelical disaster—the failure of the evangelical world to stand for truth as truth. There is only one word for this—namely accommodation: the evangelical church has accommodated to the world spirit of our age.[13]

The moral weakness of the church speaks of the moral weakness of the men of the church.

Are these Christian heroes and male leaders real men?

Even the Men Are Searching

Bombarded by conflicting messages about manhood lobbed by various camps throughout the culture, men today are left guessing about their masculinity and about their roles. These days, a lot of men are asking, "What is a 'real man'?"

The Christian author and lecturer Edwin Lewis Cole comments at length about this problem in his new book, *On Becoming a Real Man*:

> Movies, television, and entertainment give a perception of men as either stupid bunglers or super-macho heroes. Few models of manhood exist anywhere in between. Even "family" television programs show ineffective men depending on competent women to help them through life.[14]

Based on his experiences with tens of thousands of men in America and around the world, Cole adds:

> In conferences, conventions, and radio and television programs wherever I have ministered to men, one basic question consistently pops up: What is a real man?[15]

The confusion is real. Apparently gone are the days when "men were men and women were women" because no one is exactly sure anymore what defines a man (or a woman, for that matter). Beer commercials and cigarette advertisements routinely portray men as physically "tough," a little bit aloof, and usually driven by sexual desires—the "macho" man. The feminist movement, on the other hand, has been saying that real men should be intimate and open with their feelings and should learn to talk face to face—the "soft" male.[16]

The male "identity crisis" is apparent in the work world as well. If a certain vocation, say the heavy construction industry, has been historically defined as a male domain, and then the day comes when a women replaces you on the job, chances are you are going to feel some insecurity. Rightly or wrongly, you are likely to experience an emotional sense of gender instability. In your confusion the question then becomes: "What innate qualities do I uniquely possess as a man?"

Adding insult to injury, a new wave of sexual harassment suits and a new civil rights bill, allowing female "victims" to collect if they can prove their case, may change the way we were all told the "dating game" was played. *Time* magazine candidly notes:

> How are men to know what the rules are when they appear to be ever changing? At what point does misun-

derstanding become a crime? If the charges prove false, how does a man retrieve his good name?[17]

Concurrently New York's highest state court has ruled that women may go "topless" in public, striking down a former law. Within days of the decision, two women in one city smeared paint over their breasts and danced without tops in a downtown Main Street window as part of an "art display." Other women quickly took advantage of the ruling, riding their bikes to shop at downtown stores "topfree."[18] The question returns: what happens if men look? Is this sexual harassment?

The confusion is not one that affects the secular community only. Even leadership within the Christian Church seems to be baffled about unique maleness. In an exhaustive treatise on the subject, the Christian authors John Piper and Wayne Grudem add their insights:

> The sexual turmoil of our culture is not surprising when we discover that our best Christian thinkers claim not to know what masculinity and femininity are, and yet acknowledge that these are among the most profound aspects of personhood.[19]

Conclusion: A Crisis in American Manhood

In this chapter we have searched for a real man. By looking at the crisis in the state, family, and church, I have introduced the idea that what is ailing America is a fundamental crisis in American manhood. You may feel I have overdramatized the situation by focusing on some of the data we would rather not think about, but for the most part, it is becoming increasingly clear that finding genuine virility in America is not as easy as it used to be. In sports and in the media; in local, state, and national government; in the home and in the church; in business and voluntary associations— everywhere we look we see insufficiency in men. Yes, we all know of someone whom we have looked up to as a model of true masculinity, but the pool of national virility is getting dangerously low. And the problem is not getting better, it is getting worse. Restoring a rotting culture will ultimately require the restoration of men.

Until we address the adversity in the souls of men, we will continue to crumble as a nation.

2.

Rufio Is Dead

> *Behold, I am going to send you Elijah the prophet before the coming of the great and terrible day of the LORD. And he will restore the hearts of the fathers to their children, and the hearts of the children to their fathers, lest I come and smite the land with a curse.*

Malachi 4:5,6

The men of our generation have grown up with inadequate fathering, and this has caused both men and society to stumble. Like a modern-day parable, Steven Spielberg's recent film *Hook* bears a poignant message for the men of our day. But be prepared, gentlemen, if you decide to watch it. It is a comedy, and your teen-agers and little children will laugh, but you may cry. I believe the message of the movie was summed up in a single dramatic scene. The story goes this way:

Peter Pan has now grown up and has two children—Jack, about twelve, and Maggie, who is maybe seven. He is a busy executive whose career has progressively dominated his time, leaving his children, especially Jack, feeling resentful and angry. He and his wife, Moira, are visiting Wendy (who has also now grown into an old woman) in London when Captain Hook kidnaps Peter's kids in an attempt to lure him back to Never Never Land for a rematch of the fight that cost Hook his left hand.

Peter, whose name is now Peter Banning, has lost all memory of his days as Peter Pan. Born an orphan, he had been the leader of the Lost Boys in Never Never Land before falling in love with Wendy's niece, Moira, and deciding to stay in the "real world." As Peter anxiously contemplates the mysterious disappearance of his children, Tootles, one of the original Lost Boys who is now old and a seemingly senile man, brings a peculiar message in verse to Peter as the story begins to build momentum:

Have to fly
Have to fight
Have to crow
Have to save Maggie,
Have to save Jack
Hooooooookkk . . . is back

Upon his reluctant return to Never Never Land (He was dragged there by Tinkerbell.), Peter discovers that in order to regain his ability to *fly* and *fight* and *crow* he must find his "happy thought." After a lengthy and agonizing search through the recesses of his memory, he finally falls upon the scene in his mind of his son's birth. Instantly, explosive joy fills his soul as he locks onto the "happy thought" of being a father, and in so doing he begins to rise into the air and commences to soar powerfully and majestically like an eagle through the spectacular mountains and over the scenic waters of Never Never Land.

Meanwhile, Rufio, one of the older orphans, has been the fearless leader of the Lost Boys while Peter Pan was gone. A tough, go-it-alone type, Rufio is the "I-don't-need-a-father-or-any-man" king of the Lost Boys. This is the macho man of Never Never Land, a classic favorite for the fatherless.

Peter leads the Lost Boys in a successful battle against the evil pirates (To the orphans, all grown-ups are men, and all men are pirates.). Captain Hook and "Pan" prepare to duel when Peter hears his daughter cry from a tower window, "Daddy, save me!" Peter flies off to rescue Maggie, and as he does, Rufio decides to take on Hook—alone!

Rufio, about fifteen, engages Hook with fierce determination and tremendous fighting skill. They struggle up one ship deck and down another in a tense and protracted confrontation. And then it happens. In a flurry of clashing swords, Rufio accidentally drops his weapon and in an instant is run through by Hook, even as Peter is returning to the scene. Pan catches Rufio as he falls, and Rufio utters his last words in Peter's arms: "Do you know what I wish?" He says, in a hushed tone, "I wish I had a dad like you!" With those words Rufio breathes his last.

Rufio is dead now, killed without a father to protect him. Killed by the curse of the fatherless.

Anatomy of a Curse

From Adam until today, the enemy of our souls has attempted to separate sons (and daughters) from their fathers before the appointed time, before the time when the work of the father is complete in the young man. Satan's evil plot to separate the first Adam from his Father succeeded, handing mankind a curse as part of our social genetic code. But the second Adam resisted the devil and was not separated from His Father, therefore breaking the curse, even the social code of "fatherlessness."

Yet in every society that rejects the biblical view of life and culture, the curse of the fatherless will return. It is Satan's choice strategy for bringing the nations low. It is a root cause for nearly every element of social decay. This demonic strategy has been advanced in America as well. As we have drifted further from the biblical foundations for society, we have become increasingly vulnerable to this debilitating phenomenon.

The Missing Father

But what does it mean to be orphaned, or fatherless? Certainly everyone has a biological father. Somewhere you and I have a dad who brought each of us into existence, biologically speaking. The orphan, then, is not one who has no father, but rather one whose father is *missing*. This may mean a total physical absence as through death or desertion, or it may mean the father's presence is so inconsequential or so detrimental that he may as well be absent. Whether on site or gone, the father is not fulfilling his three-fold obligation to his children—provision, protection, and love.

As an orphan the son has no one to lead him into manhood, a process that cannot be done by those who have never been a man. This means that mothers, brothers and sisters, or other orphans cannot perform the task, no matter how deeply they may love the young man and want him to grow up. With this definition in mind, we can start to recognize the depth to which we live in a fatherless society. With one-third of the nation's children now living apart from one biological parent (usually the dad) and with 60 percent of America's children spending part of their childhood in a single-parent household, we can begin to see the size of the problem.[1]

In analyzing the data, we must remember that if 60 percent of all first-time marriages end in divorce, a nearly equal amount of our population will be raised without their real fathers because custody of the children is granted to the mothers in 90 percent of the cases.[2] Even if the wife remarries, the son will still not have his own father, but rather a step-father. Though many step-dads do a great job, the unfortunate reality is that raising a step-son where there is little or no natural bonding is hard work, and many men in these situations are not faring well. Surprisingly, some researchers are now convinced that children raised in step-families actually fare worse than those raised in single-parent homes.[3] The Brady Bunch made it look easy, but in real life it can be a difficult task.

This means that only about 40 percent of our children will spend the majority of their childhood growing up with their own fathers. This alone is a tragedy, but the bad news is not over yet.

Many fathers who *are* keeping their marriages together (the 40 percent group) have come from "fatherless" backgrounds themselves. Roughly half of us were never really trained in what it means to be a good father, at least not by our own dads. Though many men have acquired parenting skills from some other source, I am hearing more and more men admit that they are "learning on the job."

Because of this we see many parents raising their third or fourth child differently than they did their first two. In this scenario the older children become experiments in parenting! The parents later vow not to repeat the mistakes they made with the older children. "We get better at this as we go" may sound like a nice idea, but in reality, the parents' lack of parenting skill to begin with is part of the curse. Men were never taught by their fathers what it means to be a "Kingdom Dad." The implications for the children who were the guinea pigs are incredible.

Looking at the data as a whole, then, we can begin to put together the picture that the majority of the men in our culture are in some measure fatherless. At best maybe 20 percent of us men were raised by a full-stature godly man who truly knew the way to manhood and was willing to show us the path; the true figure is probably closer to 10 percent. The rest of us struggle with a less than adequate fathering background that ranges from absolutely horrific to mildly bad.

Inception of a Curse

The modern origins of the fatherless curse can be traced back a mere 150 years to the Industrial Revolution. For the first time in our nation's history, we began to see a wholesale separation of fathers from their sons (and daughters) by the massive exodus from the farm to the factory. We have not yet recovered from the father-son relational breakdown that occurred in the middle part of the nineteenth century.

Much has been written on this subject from both biblical and psychological perspectives. A significant work on the topic was accomplished by the Christian author Weldon Hardenbrook in the book *Missing from Action*. About the effects of the Industrial Revolution on the home he writes:

This dramatic transition literally jolted the role of men in America. Once farmers, and the children of farmers, these men exchanged work around their homes and families for new occupations in factories. And in most cases this new situation required men to leave their homes for long periods of time. Men began to lose their grip on who they were.[4]

Later he adds that, "For all practical purposes, American fatherhood was dead."[5]

From the more philosophical and humanistic camp comes the recent famed work, *Iron John: A Book About Men*, by the author and poet Robert Bly. In his preface Bly weighs in with the same assessment of the historical root of the modern fatherless dilemma:

The grief in men has been increasing steadily since the start of the Industrial Revolution, and the grief has reached a depth now that cannot be ignored.[6]

Before this point in our history, agrarian culture kept fathers and sons in close proximity throughout childhood and young adulthood. By about age seven, the young boy would begin to spend more time with his father in the fields and less time with his mother in the house. Working hand-in-hand with his dad, the son would begin to learn the stuff of manhood. The spirit of his father would be imparted to him as they worked together. But also being able to watch his dad interact with his mother in this joint business of the family farm, or the family-owned blacksmith shop, or the general store, the young lad would learn what it meant to be a husband. Nevertheless, the Industrial Revolution largely brought this generational transfer of manhood to an end.

In the black community, it was the act of forced slavery that initially parted many fathers and sons. On the auction block there were no guarantees that a man's wife or children would be included in the "sale." Whole families would often be split apart in this devilish social system. But since the signing of the Thirteenth Amendment in 1865, which abolished slavery, the black family has continued to suffer attack. The public assistance programs of Roosevelt's "New Deal" of the early 1930s have taken a bad situation and made it worse. The system actually rewards mothers for having children out of wedlock, paying them more money for having more children. At the same time, these fatherless families are financially penalized if the dad does return home. As a result, the rate of fatherlessness among black children is more than double that among white children.[7] It is my deep conviction that the advanced fatherless condition we see in the black community and the tragic impact this has had on the black family and culture is a foreshadow of where the white community is headed if there is not significant intervention.

It is observable throughout the history of cultures that Satan seeks to break apart the father-son bond and relationship. He knows that this single act will foster the deterioration of manhood and the eventual breakdown of that society's leadership and stability more than any other. Sometimes he uses the literal destruction of men through wars, while in other situations some demonically inspired social "ism," such as communism, takes the children from their fathers. Even feminism, through the promotion and passage of no-fault divorce laws, has furthered the tearing of the father-son bond. With each passing generation since the Industrial Revolution, the national reservoir of manliness has dropped lower and lower—we are at a crisis point now. The corporate pool of virility has dipped precariously below the minimum level needed for our nation to function properly.

The Father-Wounded Man

A good or great father brings health and wholeness. A bad father or no father at all inflicts a wound.

The recent film *Boyz n the Hood*, which tracks the life of a young black man growing up in a south Los Angeles neighborhood, has become yet another helpful cinematic parable for the man seeking to understand the impact of being raised without a father. The movie opens to the background sounds of police sirens, women screaming, and semi-automatic weapons being fired. The terrified voice of a little black boy yells, "They shot my brother, they shot my brother!" while the following words are emblazed across the big screen:

One out of every twenty-one black American males will be murdered.

A moment later these words appear:

Most will die at the hands of another black man.

Growing up without a godly father cripples the man. In some cases, as with Rufio, it can actually kill him. *Boyz n the Hood* has dramatically captured this devastating reality as it affects the black community. The film depicts a single black father struggling to raise his son amidst the hatred, anger, perverted sex, and violent rage of the streets. The message of the movie is simple but powerful: Out of the three boys featured, the two fatherless boys across the street were both murdered by senseless street violence; the boy with a father survived.

Modern psychologists have referred to the outcome of the fatherless estate as a "father-wound," and I think this term is helpful.

Disinherited Without the Father

What happens to a man who is raised fatherless? How does he fare in life as an adult? First, let us look at what the fatherless man lacks.

The popular notion is that a boy without a dad will lack a role model, and perhaps this is true. Nevertheless, I have come to see that something related but much deeper is actually missing. Without a dad there is no transference of the father's virility, his actual maleness. He does not simply model manhood for the son, but he actually gives it to him via episodes together in the work and play of life.

In a recent PBS documentary with Bill Moyers called "A Gathering of Men," Robert Bly talks at length about this phenomenon, saying that the substance of manhood is passed from the father to his son as they stand near each other. So we could say that the male spirit, or male nature, is hard to come by for the fatherless man.

Such a young man will also be short on encouragement and approval. This is the stuff that nurtures the soul and gives it strength. Consider what one wise Father said about His Son in a public setting: "This is my beloved Son, in whom I am well pleased" (Matt. 3:17b). Can you imagine the impact on the young man who hears his father declare his worth in public over and again? Rare are the occasions these days when a father stands in church, or at a school event, or even over the dinner table with guests and praises his son in front of God and everybody. Yet this is the food the soul feasts on.

If the son never hears words of affirmation and praise from his dad, he is likely to shrivel up and die emotionally; the father-wound will take his life. Deep insecurities in men are often the result of never having a father's approval and encouragement.[8]

There are many other deficiencies in the life of a fatherless man. The possible voids include a lack of being challenged or of being called up to something great; a deficit of direction or a sense of aimlessness for having no one to follow; the correlating lack of accountability that normally comes with being challenged; and a shortage of hope for having no one to place hope in. In general, the fatherless man experiences a scarcity of resources in the broadest sense. He is defunded and disinherited. Within the tripartite realms of his spirit, soul, and body, the man runs short on everything needed to prosper. In many cases he may actually be handed a growing debt of these life-giving substances instead of his rightful inheritance. And so we hear many fatherless men lament, "My father never gave me a thing."

During a break at a seminar I was presenting not long ago, a young man, still in his early thirties, asked if he could speak with me. After some small talk, Ron began to zero in on something of real importance to him. With his brow knit and looking off into the distance, he began to share the tragic experience of being sexually abused by his own father. Fighting back tears he passionately asked, "How can I lead a family and become a Kingdom Man with this unbearable pain in my soul?"

From the young boy who never had a father at all to the middle-aged man whose memory of his father was that of a distant man sleeping behind a newspaper in the living room, many men suffer from the "father-wound." Some were injured through what the father did—physical, sexual, or emotional abuse—while others were harmed by what their father did not do—protect, provide, and love. In either case, the problem appears to be widespread. One expert in the field of psychotherapy and men's issues believes that the majority of men have experienced this wound in some measure:

> Most of us men bear deep wounds from our relationships with our fathers. We did not experience having them available and accessible as we were growing up. Whether they were disciplinarians or passive, uninvolved bystanders, what we each got was only a piece of our fathers.[9]

While this does not excuse men from being held accountable for their own behavior, it has become my conviction that the wound men have suffered from being fatherless has become a *primary* gash in the soul of the American culture. For most men the pain and suffering have become intolerable.

Society Is Wounded Too

What many Americans consider to be our most significant cultural problems are actually only the symptoms or manifestations of the real problem—the curse of having no fathers. A close examination of some of the key issues facing our nation reveals the underlying roots of fatherlessness.

Delinquency and Crime

A look at some hard facts: 60 percent of violent rapists come from single parent homes.[10] "Approximately 70 percent of juveniles in long-term correctional facilities did not live with their fathers growing up."[11] "The literature indicates that delinquents are more likely to come from father-absent homes."[12] Furthermore, even in homes where the father is present, delinquency is more likely to occur where there is a "poor child-father relationship."[13] According to one researcher, cultures in which boys have less opportunity to interact with their fathers have a greater frequency of theft and personal crimes. They also discovered that boys without fathers will at some point exhibit "extreme masculine behavior" (e.g., crime).[14] "A Michigan State University study of adolescents who committed homicides found that 75 percent of them were from broken homes."[15]

The purpose of reporting these statistics is not to remove from blame the perpetrators of crime but to warn of more incidents if the poor father-child relationship is not addressed. These statistics, and many more that could be added, lead to the conclusion that the development of virtue in men is intrinsically tied to their relationship to their fathers—if it is intact and healthy, they will score higher in traditional measures of moral development (e.g., be less prone to cheating, stealing, and lying) and will be much less likely to get into trouble later in life. If the father is absent or the father-son relationship is poor, the boys will more likely be delinquent.

Abortion, Teen Pregnancy, and Infanticide

Fatherless girls are more likely to become sexually active earlier than those growing up with fathers.[16] Why is this so? Could it be that at an age when young girls need the attention and affection of their fathers the most, their dads are unable to provide it because they are missing? Could it be that when the young lady is reaching out for the approval and attention of a father who she dreams will say, "My, look you're beautiful tonight," there is no father in the home to utter these precious words?

Gary Bauer, head of the Family Research Council in Washington, D.C., argues that the father plays a vital role in preserving the sexual purity of his daughters.

> For daughters a father is a source of love and comfort
> that can help her avoid surrendering her virtue in a
> fruitless search for love through premarital sex.[17]

When a young lady is cut off from the soul food of fatherly affirmation, it appears that she gets very "hungry." In this situation, it is not hard to understand why she falls prey so easily to the promises of "love" from a young man. She is starving emotionally for male attention and will gladly feast at any man's table.

Put fatherless girls together with fatherless boys and the result is disastrous since the latter are also more likely to become sexually active sooner in life. Furthermore, they are less likely to be responsible for their actions because of their immaturity. When a young man gets his girlfriend pregnant and he is, say, fifteen-years old, is he likely to encourage her to give the child birth? Is he likely to promise to protect her, provide for her, and love her for the rest of his life? Is he likely to commit himself to the doctor's bills and to the nighttime feedings and to the changing of diapers? The pressures of his selfish peer culture combined with his underdeveloped level of responsibility often entice him to take the easy way out—abortion.

Looking at the abortion tragedy from another perspective, we see that certain physicians—products of our fatherless society themselves—willingly provide the means for these women to abort. Why? Because it is profitable. Even the political process is affected by the lack of fathering. One of the planks in President Clinton's election campaign was a commitment to sign the so-called "Freedom of Choice Act" (FOCA). This legislation would make killing unborn children legal in all three trimesters and would bar state legislatures from putting any restriction upon the abortion trade in their home state. Many, if not most, reading this book would agree that this is a cowardly and barbaric act on the part of our president. What many reading this book may not realize, though, is that Mr. Clinton was raised completely without his father.

Why do some men perform abortions, even though they know full well a baby will die? The "it's-just-a-blob-of-tissue" rhetoric has fallen in serious disrepute since the advent of ultrasound imaging and other devices that have allowed us to see the unborn *in utero*. The rationale has now switched to the "quality of life" ethic and the "right to terminate." One honest abortionist openly acknowledges abortion is the taking of human life:

> It's a form of life. To deny that [life] is to kill. This has to be killing. The question becomes, "Is this kind of killing justifiable?" In my own mind, it is justifiable, but only with the informed consent of the mother. It's better to say, "This is a life, albeit an early life." Give it that kind of respect and then make the decision.[18]

Justifiable killing? This admission by someone who has sworn to uphold the Hippocratic Oath is incredible in our day of supposed evolved civilization. But when the moral underpinnings are destroyed because of a lack of godly fathering, as we have seen in the statistics of moral development above, it becomes a noble thing to aspire to the high calling of becoming a "health care provider" (providing, of course, that the money is there).

And what of the abortion rights advocates, those female leaders who trumpet the cause of killing our offspring? Does fatherlessness play a role here? In her recent book, *Revolution from Within: A Book of Self-Esteem*, the abortion champion Gloria Steinem, also called "the world's most famous Feminist," tells of being abandoned by her father and left in abject poverty to care for her mentally ill mother at the age of ten. Is it any wonder this avowed celibate would have difficulty trusting men? Is it any wonder she would devote herself to promoting the idea that a woman must control her "own body," even if that control would sometimes cost that woman the life of her own unborn child? Is it any wonder she would play a vital role in attacking the so-called "male-dominated" society we all hear so much about in these days?

The feelings of anger and bitterness toward men run deep in the militant Feminist camp, and the lack of godly fathering is likely at the root. Randall Terry, the founder of the pro-life activist group Operation Rescue, has observed this phenomenon in his interactions with Feminist leaders:

> Most feminists readily admit, in their writings and personal conversations, that they possess a root of bitterness stemming from a relationship with a man who betrayed his responsibilities as either a father or a husband. This obviously places some of the blame on arrogant, foolish men who have committed evils—some of them very significant—against women.[19]

Teen pregnancy, infanticide, and the killing of preborn babies is traceable from many angles to a lack of true men in the culture. From the emotional vacuum that fuels the skyrocketing teen pregnancy phenomenon to the man-hating solutions of the feminist agenda and the child-killing "services" of the male-dominated abortion industry, the conspicuous absence of *real men*—men who were fathered—is fatally evident.

Crippling Immaturity in Leadership

Watching the presidential debates of the 1988 election between George Bush and Mike Dukakis, I remember noticing that the mannerisms and behavior of Dukakis somehow reminded me more of a young boy quarreling on the school playground than that of a sophisticated grown man debating the national and international issues of the day. It seemed to me that Dukakis was trying hard to act mature, but failing. A faint sense of insecurity and a need to prove himself was my distinct impression. Bush, on the other hand, seemed more confident, somehow more grown-up. I wondered about this for some time. Later I discovered that Mr. Dukakis was raised by a rigid workaholic father, who, according to Michael's mother, spent too much time tending to his career. George Bush, on the other hand, had a strong and healthy fathering background.

It is my observation that the emotional development of a fatherless man can become quite stunted. Depending on the age he was when his father left, and the role of other men in his life, among other factors, this emotional immaturity can range from severe to only slightly noticeable.

An eight-year-old boy is not expected to demonstrate the same degree of emotional maturity and self-control that we expect from adult men. And yet what happens if a man hits an emotional maturity ceiling equal to that of a ten-year-old which he never overcomes because this is the age when things broke down between him and his dad? Furthermore, what if an eight-year-old "boy" in a older man's body is the governor of your state or your congressional representative?

As we have seen in chapter 1, part of the damage to our men is that they are having difficulty in leadership on all levels. This is nowhere more evident than in the political arena. From the White House to the county legislature, fatherless men fill the civil arena, and they attempt to lead from their place of woundedness and immaturity.

But the effects are not limited to the visible pedestal of political leadership. The impact of this immaturity reaches every dimension of the community. Business leaders like Mr. Turner bring the wounds into the commercial world, while other men simply struggle with leading a family. The next time you watch politicians debate, think of the school yard comparison and see if you can tell the fathered from the fatherless.

There are many cultural issues we could explore—poverty, sexual exploitation, sexual perversion, racial tension and urban turmoil, drug abuse, declining productivity, environmental concerns, and so forth—and we would see that the root issue in every area can be traced back to a lack of fathers in the land.

One researcher, referred to by the *Boston Globe* as an "impeccably credentialed liberal," shocked the world of political correctness in a recent essay dealing with the fallout of divorce and the absence of fathers in childrearing. In an *Atlantic Monthly* article entitled, "Dan Quayle Was Right," Barbara Dafoe Whitehead takes the reader through more than twenty statistics-jammed pages of depressing analysis about the unbelievable devastation family breakdown and fatherless homes are having on the American social fabric. She summed up with these words:

> Family disruption would be a serious problem even if it affected only individual children and families. But its impact is far broader. Indeed, it is not an exaggeration to characterize it as a central cause of many of our most vexing social problems.[20]

> It dramatically weakens and undermines society, placing new burdens on schools, courts, prisons, and the welfare system. These new families [single-parent or step-families] are not an improvement on the nuclear family, nor are they even just as good, whether you look at outcomes for children or outcomes for society as a whole.[21]

An article from the American Family Association put it this way: "Almost every vexing social problem is related to family dissolution."[22]

As the father goes, so goes the family. And as the family goes, so goes the nation.

The Church Is Wounded Too

Not long ago I had the opportunity to speak at a men's gathering in a northeastern city. Toward the end of my message, I shared the idea of becoming "sons" of the older men in the faith as part of the process of confronting our own fatherless condition (a concept we will deal with at length in chapters 4 and 5). Then I challenged the men to respond to this call by rising to their feet. All across the meeting hall, men slowly began to rise and declare their desire to be "re-fathered" by other Christian men. They had begun to see that this was an essential part of becoming a Kingdom Man.

After I finished speaking and had taken my seat, the senior pastor came forward to close the meeting. His remarks started innocently enough, but before long I noticed he was systematically attempting to undermine the core of my message. He reiterated the need to be healed of the father-wound but emphasized that all that was necessary was prayer.

Shortly after the meeting ended, I took the pastor aside and said, "Dan, why did you do that? Didn't you understand the point—that what men are emotionally hungering for is other men, not prayer?" Looking down at the floor, he replied, "I knew full well what you meant and I agree with you, but the more you shared, the more afraid I became. In fact," he said, "at one point I began to pray that our men wouldn't hear your message, because if they did they may begin to ask from me something that I can't give them." And then, he turned and looked straight at me and sighed, "For you see, David, I too am a fatherless man."

It appears that the ratio of father-wounded men in the body of Christ roughly reflects that of our secular culture. Between the bar on one corner and the church on the other, there is not much difference in regard to the percentage of the men affected by the curse. Not surprisingly, we may actually have a higher level in the local church because many of the wounded fatherless have looked to us for healing and settled in our ranks. Orphaned men fill our pulpits, and they sit on our deacon's boards. I know of several congregations where nearly every man in the church, including the senior leader, is, to some degree, in this camp.

In my estimation the tragic fatherless estate of the churches in America is the major cause for our lack of spiritual potency. Our souls may be "born again," but our emotions are still dying from the injuries of our upbringing. Like the walking wounded, we are unable to stand up like real men and "fight the good fight."

The Lack of Moral Courage

This woundedness is likely the fundamental reason why many Christian men—leaders and laymen—lack the moral courage and the will to resist the relentless advances of the dark kingdom. Our institutional unwillingness to confront the abortion holocaust is a prime example of this.

In my travels, speaking to churches and challenging Christians to become active in stemming the horror of abortion, I have noticed that more women than men generally respond to my message. It is not that the men disagree with the idea that Christians should take an active stand against this evil trade. Rather, it appears that they lack the *will* to rise up. They seem, as a whole, more passive than the women when it comes to rescuing babies and mothers from this hellish social lie. Indeed, in my own city, more than two-thirds of the active pro-life leaders are women, and the same holds true on the national level.

The reasons for this are numerous and complex, but I believe a root issue here is an unwillingness to act like real men—men who are willing to confront the true spiritual force behind the death industry. Allow me to explain.

Historically, child-sacrifice (now called abortion) has always arisen from what could be called a "Jezebel" spirit. The figure Jezebel in the Bible sought to control and dominate her weak husband, Ahab (1 Kings 16-22). Although he was the "head of the house" as well as the ruler of the northern kingdom of Israel, Jezebel called the shots. She also initiated ritual child-killing. Like Ahab, our orphaned men have become too afraid, too weak, or simply too passive to resist child-killing in our day. The cost of fighting on the abortion front seems too high a price to be paid because it means confronting the demonic force behind the killing.

Whenever men refuse to lead or become incapable of leading, they create a "leadership vacuum" in the home, at church, and in the community. This hole will be filled by something—children or women will assume the reins of leadership (Isa. 3:12). Often when women fill the leadership spots left vacant by men, they become spiritually vulnerable to a Jezebel-like spirit, which is to say the temptation to rule over their weak husbands becomes great. The Christian mom who takes her children to church week after week, year after year, while her "saved" husband sleeps in or stays home to "rest," knows full well that it is her husband's job, not hers, to be the spiritual head of the home. Yet he is unwilling to lead. I regularly encounter scores of women who lament that their husbands refuse to be the spiritual leaders in the home. They share stories of male passivity and weak wills.

Mixed into this equation is the factor that countless Christian women were themselves raised without fathers. Others were brought up by ungodly dads, some by fathers who abused them. Even many of those who spent their younger years in a Christian home were likely to be raised by a dad who did poorly because he was fatherless himself. Because of this many of the women pulled into the leadership spots in the family and society already carry resentment against men and bring this pain into their role as replacement leader.

Of course, this does not always have to happen. The woman Deborah is a striking example of how a godly woman filled the leadership shoes left by a man, and yet she never gave in to a corrupt attitude of despising men or lording it over them (Judg. 4). Nevertheless, many times foul and demonic powers prey on women who have been pulled into the leadership vacuum created by the abandonment of men. Because of the shortcomings in fathers and husbands, a great number of our Christian women have become susceptible to the demonic influence of an ungodly spirit. The object of this evil presence is to convince women (and sometimes men) to resist male authority on many levels. The goal becomes to control—to eventually rule over—men. This is clearly the spirit behind the modern Feminist movement.

Hardenbrook notes that once this control has been embraced by women, even if only on a small level, it is hard to give up:

> I cannot begin to relate how many women I have heard over the years talking about the need for their hus-bands to be the spiritual leaders of the home. Then to my surprise, when their husbands began to take that responsibility, many of these same women resented it. Why? Because when men begin to establish spiritual leadership, they threaten women's role of moral su-premacy. Women have been schooled in Victorian thought, and to them, losing the spiritual leadership in the home means losing control in the raising of the children.[23]

Like Ahab, a great number of "kings" are unwilling to confront this demonic influence because they are afraid of offending the women upon whom it preys. Others see it but are simply too weak to do anything. Understanding this we can now begin to see why the men of the church refuse to confront abortion. How can they stand up to the Jezebel-backed abor-tion industry on a city-wide basis when they have not yet learned to confront that demonic influence in their own homes? It will never happen.

Some men reading this may conclude, then, that "strong women" must be the problem. Careful, gentlemen, you are about to make a tragic mistake. Before you charge off and do something rash, let me gently but firmly remind you of a pivotal truth: "Jezebel" is only welcome in a place where "Ahab" is king. The problem is not with the women; the problem is with the men. Our less-then-adequate response as men to the abortion holocaust epitomizes the dilemma of weak men in the church.

Revenge of the Fatherless

Now that we have explored the wound that men and soci-ety have experienced because of the breakdown in fathering, it will be helpful to look at a related phenomenon we could call the "revenge of the fatherless."

When a young boy growing up is mistreated, ignored, or abandoned by his dad, his resulting wounds may give birth to the powerful force of resentment. And this anger does not dissipate with time; rather it seems to actually grow as if incubated in the hothouse of the soul. A father's unkind statement—"You jerk, can't you ever do anything right?"—gets replayed a thousand times in the young boy's mind as he grows older. With each playback of those piercing words, the original pain and hurt become magnified. Inside he knows he loves his father, but a conflicting anger continues to build.

For some men this unrelenting animosity produces a passion for revenge, and the target of their attack is the father figure, meaning the generation of men that are older. Bly says that a man may

> take revenge on the remote father by making all adult men look like fools. They attack the respect for masculine integrity that every father, underneath, wants to pass on to his grandchildren and great-grandchildren.[24]

This is generational warfare. The retaliation may take on many forms. It can be conscious or subconscious, overtly aggressive or passive. It can be active early in life or lie dormant for many years. In any case the compulsion to act on this anger is real.

It seems to me that a great number of men spend decades of their lives seeking to prove their fathers wrong—wrong about them and wrong about life in general. The young man whose dad repeatedly put him down finally reaches adulthood and declares, "I am not stupid! I will amount to something! Just you watch and see! I'll show you who's stupid!" And so he drives himself mercilessly to perform at his career only to harm his own family by his physical and emotional absence.

Another man, who was physically beaten by an overbearing and controlling father, vows never to spank his children. Later he finds that his "hands off" approach produces disastrous results in his own children. Still another, whose father abandoned him and his mother when he was six, ends up regarding all older men as unfaithful. These and many other subtle forms of reprisal can often consume the best years of a man's life.

Ironically, some men appear to "get even" with their dads by becoming just like them. This is not a conscious decision, of course, but it accomplishes the same devastating results. This tragic form of revenge was powerfully illustrated in the popular song, "Cat's in the Cradle." In this song the busy father never takes enough time for his son as the boy is growing up, and yet his son continues to idolize him. In the final verse, the son is now grown and married, and the father calls and wants to get together, but the son is now too busy. The father hangs up, lamenting that his son had grown up just like him.

How many elderly gentlemen live alone in the cold environment of a nursing home, suffering from this form of retribution? How many others never even receive a phone call or a visit from their sons who live just across town? In America more phone calls are made on Mother's Day than on any other day of the year. Father's Day, on the other hand, may be more reflective of the revenge of the fatherless, for it is, annually, the day of the most collect calls.

Some of the revenge stays within the family circle, and some gets played out in the public arena. Remember, as I noted earlier, eight out of ten men are in some measure fatherless in our day. What happens, then, when a dozen of these men become the senior editors of the nation's major newspapers or the television networks? What happens if one becomes the owner of CNN? What impact is made on our values and perspectives in America if some of these men use their platforms in life to convince us all that their dad's views on life were wrong? Often by accident, these wounded and hurting men take their cases against their fathers into the public square of ideas.

The result of all this revenge? Modern America.

Conclusion: America Is under a Curse

Everywhere we look we see the manifestation of the curse of no fathers. If we know what we are looking for, we will recognize the powerful and devastating revenge that fatherless men are unwittingly taking out on themselves and all of society.

Surely we will not last long under this curse. The good news is that we don't have to.

Epilogue to Part I

Accepting the Call

Everywhere we turn we see that a curse has been released in America. Since the time of the Industrial Revolution until now, we have been dying because of the enemy's efforts to separate fathers and sons. The resulting father-wound has caused men and society to suffer greatly, and now our culture is being tormented by the revenge of the fatherless. The saved and the unsaved are affected. There is no escaping the reaches of this terrible scourge.

But there is hope! In fact, there is great hope! We have taken two long chapters to search for some real men and to explore the curse of the fatherless. Now it is time to turn the page from the darkness of the problem to the light of God's solutions. It is time to accept the call—the call to confront the curse and become a *King's Man*.

Part II

Journey to Manhood

3.

In Search of the King

*And because you are sons, God has sent forth the Spirit of His
Son into our hearts, crying, "Abba! Father!"*

Galatians 4:6

At the very moment a boy enters the world, he begins a
long journey toward the King—the Father God of the Bible.
The steps in this trek were carefully designed by the Father
Himself to lead us into His royal chambers. Through each
phase of this earthly pilgrimage, the boy is assigned tutors who
help guide him toward the mark of reaching His presence.

As a man sets out on this pilgrimage, his travels will take
him through ascending realms of authority that begin with
Mother and end in the King's throne room. He will move

higher and higher, as if internally programmed to continue his upward pursuit, until he reaches the peak—the King's presence—and becomes a "son of the King."

There are many ways we could describe the various phases of the journey. I have observed four levels or plateaus that the boy will climb "up" to and then travel through on his trip. I think the journey goes something like this:

> One day a baby boy is born and falls fast asleep. A few days later he wakes up in the kitchen with his mother. It's warm in the kitchen, and everything about Mom is very soft. She speaks softly, wears soft clothes, and her skin is soft, too.

> One day the boy sees his father walk through the kitchen, kiss his mother, and go out the front door into the fields. The same thing happens the next day, and the next.

> After a few days, the little boy leaves the kitchen and follows his dad to the porch. From here they go together into the fields of manhood. Life in the fields is much harder than in the kitchen. The boy must endure heat and cold, wind and rain, darkness, and at times a scorching sun. He gets tired sometimes, and he thinks about returning to the kitchen. But somehow he knows he must stay. Besides, he really likes being with his dad.

> Years later the boy sees a young man walk through the fields on his way to college. The next day the same thing happens except this young man is headed for boot camp training. The third day still another young man walks through the fields on his way to seminary.

> After spending many years in the fields with Dad, the young man leaves the farm and travels into the world of other men. Here he finds two or three men who offer to teach him many practical things needed for living off the farm. He misses his mother and father, and often the boy returns to the farm for a visit, but he knows he cannot stay. Soon he starts a family and takes a job in the world of men.

> On a certain day, after living in the world of men for

many years, the young man hears a voice say, "This is my son," but the voice is not that of his real father; instead he turns and sees the King. The King invites him to become his son and the boy accepts, realizing that this is what he had desired all along.

The young boy has now become a man. But not just any man. He has become the son of the King, which makes him a King's Man!

Whether we know it or not, whether we admit it or not, we are all searching for the King.

Journey to Manhood

We have seen in the first two chapters that there is an enemy of the King, Satan, who seeks to knock us off the path. He knows that it is our destiny to find the King and to do His glorious work. This could be called our Kingdom vocation, and in it we find our life and true fulfillment. Our adversary also knows that separation from the King ultimately means our death, and this is what he wants.

To understand what it means to become a *Kingdom Man*, we must first understand the process of reaching the King's presence.

Arrival of a Mama's Boy

One day a baby boy is born and falls fast asleep. A few days later he wakes up in the kitchen with his mother.

The starting spot for the expedition must be referred to as the *Mama's Boy* stage. In this place Mom is seen as the ultimate ruler! As far as the child is concerned, she holds the keys to life and death; she is his source of provision and protection; she provides most of the nurturing and care—she is the sovereign one. She is the king, at least for now. As a frail little man, the boy must totally rely upon his mother to sustain his very life.

Some mothers are not conscious of the broad and lasting impact they are having on their toddlers during this time. They assume they are simply keeping the baby fed, diapered, and rested. Even so, during these tender days in a boy's life, the mother is teaching her son his first vital character trait needed for survival—the ability to trust someone in authority. In his classic work, *Childhood and Society*, Eric H. Erikson explores this emergence of trust in the infant-mother relationship:

> The firm establishment of enduring patterns for the solution of the nuclear conflict of basic trust versus basic mistrust in mere existence is the first task of the ego, and thus first of all a task for maternal care. But let it be said here that the amount of trust derived from earliest infantile experience does not seem to depend on absolute quantities of food or demonstrations of love, *but rather on the quality of the maternal relationship*. Mothers create a sense of trust in their children by that kind of administration which in its quality combines sensitive care of the baby's individual needs and a firm sense of personal trustworthiness within the trusted framework of their culture's life style.[1] (emphasis added)

In his vulnerability an infant son has no choice but to trust mom. Mother either cares for him or he dies. If she hurts him emotionally or physically, he comes to believe that the king only brings harm and cannot be trusted. This mistrust will permeate his developing perception of authority and make it more difficult for him to trust "kings" in the future. But if she attends to her maternal mission with diligence and godly care, he learns that the king *can* be trusted. This ability to trust authority builds confidence and security in the little guy. He will need these for the days ahead. For these traits empower the growing man to reach and to climb, because he is now inclined to trust people, especially leaders, and to eventually trust God. A well-mothered man has the potential to become a trusting and trustworthy man, a faithful man. He is a *King's Man* in the making.

Consider the faithful mothers of some of the great men of God. It was said of Timothy that his mother had a sincere faith (2 Tim. 1:5). After being mentored and trained by the apostle Paul, Timothy went on to become the senior elder at the city-wide church at Ephesus. Think of the great prophet Samuel, whose mother Hannah prayed fervently for a child and, when

God answered her prayer, willingly gave him to the priest to be trained from a young age. The Bible says that she would come up each year and bring him clothes. What faithfulness to God and to her son Samuel!

Susanna Wesley, the mother of Charles and John Wesley, was one of these trustworthy maternal giants. In spite of many and great hardships—the infant deaths of ten of her nineteen children, a fire that completely destroyed their home and belongings, an attack on their home by an angry mob, and her husband's incarceration in debtor's prison—Susanna's unswerving faith and moral courage helped produce two of the Christian Church's greatest saints. She is as much a part of the grand legacy of the Church as are her two renowned sons.

In the same pattern as these outstanding mother-son duos, ideally, mom and son may bond during this time, and the little fellow will grow healthily toward the next realm of authority.

The Making of a Daddy's Boy

> After a few days, the little boy leaves the kitchen and follows his dad to the porch. From here they go together into the fields of manhood.

Somewhere between the ages of three and seven, a young boy begins to recognize that there is yet a higher authority than Mom. There is another king, and his name is Dad. It comes as an emotional shock to the son to discover that this new monarch is actually in authority over Mom. This is terribly disillusioning because the boy realizes that the one he thought was the supreme ruler—Mom—is under the rule of someone else.

This realization, of course, means that the male child is no longer at what he perceives to be the "right hand of authority," which is his heart's innate desire. Because God programmed him to seek out and locate the King, and because he has now discovered that there is a higher authority than his mother, he realizes he must move forward.

Up until this time, the youngster had often thought of Dad as some giant, sandpaper-faced barbarian who shows up at the end of the day with the express purpose of terrorizing him. All Junior knows is that this kerosene-breathed monster gets his jollies by swinging him around the room and throwing him in the air. Then he reads the paper and goes to bed.

Because of his greater size, deep voice, and hairy appearance, Dad is often viewed as a more fearful presence than Mom. I can almost hear these little fellows thinking, "You've gotta be kidding! You mean Dad's the boss? Oh no!"

Who would ever want to get close to this towering beast? And yet there is an internal compulsion that draws the son toward his father. Inside he knows that he craves to draw near to this higher authority. And so he begins his first transition—from Mama's world to Daddy's—and in so doing he embarks upon his second act of ascension toward the King.

If all has gone well in the Mama's Boy stage, the son will progressively find the courage to venture into the more dangerous world of becoming a *Daddy's Boy*. This means that the bonding with mother has been completed and his sense of personal identity and security has reached a certain maturity level. It is from the safety and emotional strength of succeeding as a Mama's Boy that he will discover the bravery to step out into the world of this new king.

The boy now begins to move closer to his father. Before the Industrial Revolution, a son would likely begin to work with Dad by about age seven. In those times he would move out of the kitchen and into the fields—from the world of women to the world of men.

This, of course, does not suggest a break from Mom. Rather, out of the strength of the maternal relationship the young man is now emotionally empowered to broaden his social horizons, a major portion of which include the father.

Alexander Mitscherlich, a German social-psychologist, explores the impact of the fatherless estate earlier in this century. In *Society Without the Father*, he notes that the mother-deprived child will have great difficulty "in gaining a growing understanding of [his] own identity through the turbulent years of development," and in his ability to make human contact as he grows older.[2] Conversely, the child whose maternal experience has been healthy will be inclined to acquire the emotional capacity to negotiate the relational challenges that lie ahead.

At this point the young boy will go in and out of the kitchen, but his focus will now become drawing closer to his father. It would be during this next decade of his life that the young lad would learn the earthy stuff of manhood, what Mitscherlich called the "basis and essentials of dependable behavior."[3] He would experience cold and heat, light and dark. Dealing with physical discomfort and learning endurance would be inevitable. Many of his fears would be confronted during this time of his development, like fear of wild animals, fear of pain, and fear of failure. During these days, the boy would become a man.

What is unique about the Daddy's Boy plateau is that the very substance of manhood seems to be poured into the young man as he works with his father. It appears that this is much more than "role modeling." A vital transfer of manhood is taking place—from one spirit to another, from one man to a second, from the father to his son, from generation to generation. Virility is being given—from one who has it to one who needs it. The vocational trade that the son learns from his father during this time is actually a secondary issue. The occupational work of the father may be different from that to which the son is ultimately called. But their spiritual vocation is identical; they are both called to Kingdom Manhood, not farming or driving heavy equipment or computer science.

During these invaluable years of his life, a man is building on the foundations laid during the maternal phase, continuing his preparation for entering the adult world. Here he discovers more about properly relating to men, women, and children. He completes the development of moral character and the acquisition of ethical values that will guide him in his dealings in the world of adults. He learns the eternal value of work, that without work we are cursed to idleness and nonproductivity. He is taught about the true nature of war and how to know when fighting is justified. In short, he is taught how to be a real man.

Successful climbers who have made it safely through the Mama's Boy and Daddy's Boy stage are now ready for the next real adventure in their odyssey.

Becoming a Man's Man

> After spending many years in the fields with Dad, the
> young man leaves the farm and travels into the world
> of other men.

During the early to mid-teen years, young men slowly
become aware of another unsettling reality—Dad is not the
King either!

Can you remember when you thought your dad was the
final say in all matters? I can. If I would get into a fight on the
playground, the first words out of my mouth would be, "I'm
gonna tell my dad!" And I believed that, in doing so, Dad
would be able to straighten that guy out. "My dad is bigger
than you," I thought, and it seldom occurred to me that my
opponent might have a dad, too. Even when I did remember
this possibility, I figured my dad was stronger than his dad. It
simply had never crossed my mind that there might be a
power or authority higher than my father.

And then it happened.

I remember the terribly frightening experience of my
father's being stopped once by a police officer for a traffic
violation. For the first time, I became aware that Dad had to
obey someone else, in this case, the police officer. I had learned
over the years to trust my mother and father, but I did not
know this policeman from Adam. How could I be sure that he
was being fair or that he would not take my dad to jail for
something he did not do? This was very unsettling, indeed.

This experience, along with several others, became like a
sledge hammer that eventually smashed my sheltered view of
reality as I realized that Dad had to answer to a higher authority!

Once this door is opened, it is hard to shut. Soon I began
to see that there were actually many authority figures in my
father's world—his boss, the police officer, the mayor, the
president, and even the pastor. I had no relationship with any
of these people, and though I was generally a trusting person,
it became obvious to me that I would need to get to know
those who were in authority in order to be secure around
them. Besides, that gut-level drive to get closer to the highest

authority possible was as strong as ever. Soon I was thinking that I must push myself forward and begin to relate to other men in the world beyond the family.

It must again be pointed out that for the young man to continue his climb upward—what I have called the Mama's Boy, Daddy's Boy, and now a *Man's Man*—he needs to experience success at each level. In other words, when he finally begins to venture out of the kitchen and onto the porch, Dad (or some other father-like figure) must be there to meet him. Without the maturity and inner strength normally developed during the important years relating to a "father," the man will likely struggle in his ascension to the next plane. Manhood, in full stature, has not yet been fully developed in him. Some men apparently become "stuck" at this stage, hitting an emotional maturity ceiling they cannot break through, at least not by themselves.

Nevertheless, let us assume that the youth continues his upward journey. He has successfully bonded with his mother, then with his father, and he is now beginning to travel out into the even more dangerous world of adult men, the realm beyond the farm. Wherever he goes ascension marks his path. If the man enters college, his goal becomes to graduate or reach a higher degree. He may enter the business world and begin climbing the corporate ladder. This is normal because he is headed toward the highest authority in the company. He may join an area church or some local social club, and in both cases the ascension will continue. In the church he will first help as an usher, then a deacon, and eventually join the governing board.

Countless men have shared with me that they have experienced a phenomenal desire to be close to the pastor. They sometimes get a little embarrassed in relating this, but it is actually healthy and natural because it reflects their desire to be close to the highest authority available. If a man becomes a politician, will he stay at the school board level? Not on your life! Before long the aspiring civil servant is running for county or state legislative posts. After many years he seeks a congressional spot and eventually even a presidential bid. So in every area of life, we see men progressing upward.

During the years spent at this place in the journey, a man learns much that his father could never teach him. Most of it, though, is technical in nature. He will learn how to do something but not why he should do it. He is taught the knowledge of life from these men whereas he should have already learned the ethical and moral guidelines from his earlier days with his father.

Emergence of the King's Man

> On a certain day, after living in the world of men for many years, the young man hears a voice say, "This is my son," but the voice is not that of his real father; instead he turns and sees the King. The King invites him to become his son, and the boy accepts, realizing that this is what he had desired all along.

By the time a man reaches thirty, he begins to notice that something very important is missing in his life. If he has progressed through each of the previous plateaus in his trip with at least a minimal amount of success, he is likely to begin to apprehend a new and very big idea.

It is at this point that he becomes acutely aware of a Supreme Authority in the realms beyond his own world. Although many men come to believe in God long before this time, and some may even become committed Christians, there is nonetheless something very different about this new knowledge. Never before has he been so aware that a Cosmic Ruler exists. Never before has this revelation been apparent. In some way it has been blocked from his thinking. But now he is keenly aware that there is a Higher Authority than all that he sees here below.

It is at this point when a man makes his final ascent toward that Ultimate Authority. At this phase he begins to reach toward the Father of the universe, the God of the Bible, the King over all other kings. A door is opened to him to enter into a special relationship with God as his Father.

It was at this age that Jesus began to relate to God as His heavenly Father. Before this He was known as the carpenter's son; at this stage He was known as the Son of God. Before this He did the work of men, but at this stage He did the work of

His Father in heaven. Before this, He submitted Himself to His earthly parents (Luke 2:51), but at this stage He looked to His Father for authority and direction. Before this He spent time as a Mama's Boy, a Daddy's Boy, and even a Man's Man, but at this stage Christ had become the first *King's Man*.

It is worthy to note that God saw fit to hold back other Kingdom men until they were thirty years old. David became king over Israel at this very age. Thirty was also the exact age that Joseph achieved before he graduated to the important post of second ruler in Egypt. We also find that the Levites were not permitted to serve before this special age. Apparently, the Father is quite willing to wait patiently for men to complete the journey to manhood before using them in His service.

The many experiences of a man's life should have been building the foundation for this special time. Everything thus far has been preparatory in nature. Each of the previous phases have been tutorial, and now the man should discover the final plateau—intimacy with his Father in the royal chambers of heaven.

It is at this place of close proximity to the King that each of us finds our marching orders. Until now we have been in training, but now we should begin to understand what all of this preparation was for. It is here that we should be able to draw close enough to the Father to actually "hear" what He wants us to do.

> The young boy has now become a man. But not just any man. He has become the son of the King, which makes him a King's Man!

Faces of the Fatherless

As we will explore more deeply in chapters to come, the goal of the journey to manhood is to become a "son of the King." After all, what creation is eagerly awaiting is the emergence of the "sons of God," generically meaning children of God, or ones who serve and submit to their Father's will (Rom. 8:19). The Journey to Manhood then is the process of finding our way to the Father's presence and entering into His will for our lives as Jesus did. If we lived in a perfect world, the above four-phase scenario would be the blessed lot of every developing boy. But, this utopian dream is not the case, of course, and the destroyer of men's souls knows the devilish implications of derailing men along the pathway to manhood, perhaps better than we do.

Having followed the ideal journey from Mama's Boy to King's Man, we must now ask ourselves some questions: What becomes of the boy on the porch whose father never arrives to lead him into the fields of manhood? What does a young man do if the father arrives but is crippled and cannot make it to the field himself? What if the father takes the boy into the field for ten minutes and then sends him back to the kitchen? What should be done if the father takes the boy into the fields only to hurt him? Tragically, most of the men reading this book will have experienced one or more of these destructive scenarios.

Many of us had fathers who never showed up at all. We were left standing on the porch of life, alone and guessing. Too many of our dads became one of the "average fathers" that Dobson and other child psychologists tell us spend less than three minutes a day with their children. Maybe our father was an assembly line worker who spent ten hours a day at the factory and his "free time" at the bar on the way home from work. Perhaps Dad was a driven executive who was too busy climbing the corporate ladder to spend much time with us. Some of our fathers were pastors or Christian leaders who put "ministry" and "serving God" before spending time with us.

Standing on the porch alone at the age of five is a horrifying experience. If "Hope deferred makes the heart sick" (Prov. 13:12), then standing on the porch alone can kill a man's soul. The feeling is terror, one's worst nightmare come true. I do not think I am overstating the case because this single traumatic element of a young boy's experience often becomes a pivotal emotional issue for the rest of his life.

Many men did not realize they were standing on the porch alone until they reached their teen-age years. Dad never came to their "football games" (or chess tournament or the school play or the marching band concert). Other men began to notice much earlier that Dad never had time to ride bikes or build model cars because he was too tired.

Some fathers stood near the porch and ridiculed their sons as they stood there alone and, in a sense, naked. Mother could not rescue the son from this torment because she was in the kitchen. The son was exposed to the demented torment of the father.

Tragically, some boys were taken into the fields by their fathers but not to the fields of manhood. These boys were abused by their dads in ways that left permanent scars on their souls.

Of course, some men never even went out to the porch because they never saw Dad walk through the kitchen, kiss the mother, and head out the front door. From as early as they can remember, they never had a dad. Or if they did have a dad, he walked through the kitchen, struck the mother, and left for good when they were five or six.

Either way they never made it the porch—they stayed in the kitchen. These men may be emotionally distant from the imagery of the "porch" because as of yet it has never occurred to them that the "porch" is the emotional and relational membrane that must be crossed in order to leave the kitchen and enter the fields of manhood. I hope this book helps these men to wish for the porch, because until a man sees the porch and wishes to cross it, he will never enter manhood.

So where does a boy turn when left abandoned on the Porch of Life? There are at least three paths that men often take when left standing on the porch alone.

Wanderings of a Wimp

The *Wimp* goes back to the kitchen. This is the fatherless man who becomes completely disillusioned with the idea of ever finding a father, and so he retreats back to the safe world of women. Because Dad failed to show up, he learns not to trust other men. He decides to live in the kitchen of his soul, the place where Mother rules, for he is most comfortable here.

I have known some Wimps who married their "mothers." These are men who seek out a wife who, for whatever reason, wants to control a man. He, of course, is looking for that type of relationship and that type of leadership. She tells him what to wear, what job to hold, what his strengths and weaknesses are, and what company to keep. Since her approval is inordinately important to his emotional security, he voluntarily submits to her authority.

Because the Wimp identifies more with his mother than his father and because he seeks her approval in a way that is imbalanced and excessive, he may be more likely to prefer a feminine appearance. He may wear his hair long and get his ear pierced. His clothing and mannerisms may also be more feminine, and he might avoid activities that are rough or dangerous. One Christian psychologist believes this is directly related to the lack of bonding with the father.

> Studies have shown that fathers who interact often with their sons and show affection to them have sons who are rated more masculine than those whose fathers are neglectful. Thus a young boy's masculinity is a function in part of the frequency and intensity of his contact with a father-figure . . . Practically everyone has known some boy who was labelled "a sissy." This child is usually neglected by his father and identifies strongly with his mother.[4]

This is not to say that every man who wears his hair long or has an earring is over reliant upon women. Some may simply prefer the "look." But it does suggest that many men may not realize the degree to which their clothing and appearance are determined by their wish to please the mother figures in their lives. In fact, it appears that a "Lady's Man" may often be little more than a grown-up Mama's Boy. This kind of man is still seeking Mother's approval, and every time the women at the bar or the office show him attention because of the way he looks or because of something "sensitive" he does, he gets the assurance that he still pleases "Mom." He often does not know how much he needs it.

The Wimp may have another problem. Many studies seem to indicate that the fatherless man who retreats to feminized mannerisms and orientation is more vulnerable to homosexuality. Based on clinical work and research with nearly one thousand homosexuals, the psychoanalyst Irving Bieber proposed that the link between the father-son breakdown and the propensity toward homosexuality is overwhelmingly evident.[5]

Another psychologist agrees with this assessment:

> Apparently, the fathers of male homosexuals don't serve as effective models for their sons. In one way or another—through either neglect, absence, passivity, or abuse—they don't extend to their sons the warm rays of love and attention necessary to encourage their burgeoning masculinity.[6]

On one level the dependency relationship many men have with their mothers or surrogate mothers is helpful because it makes the pain of the father-wound go away for awhile. But eventually it comes back. Besides, even the best mother in the world can never be your father. Nor can she lead you into the fields of manhood.

Footsteps of the Macho Man

There is another path fatherless men take, and we will call this the way of the *Macho Man*. The Macho Man decides he does not need a father or any other man; he can "go it alone." And so he jumps off the porch in desperate defiance and heads out to the fields by himself. Hardenbrook says the Macho Man is "often portrayed as an independent man who could find life very satisfying without any ties to family or others."[7]

Apparently the Macho Man thinks he can obtain from independence what only another man can give him. "Maybe I'll become a real man by lifting weights," he thinks, "or by having lots of sex, or by getting a degree all by myself, or by starting a business and becoming really successful, or by . . ." He is usually not aware until much later in life that he is expending a tremendous amount of energy attempting to prove to his father that he really does not need him.

The harder the Macho Man tries his "I'll-do-it-myself" approach, the more miserable he becomes. Progressively, he discovers that even when he succeeds at all of his self-made macho goals he is never content with the outcome. Sure, he now has a family (maybe even his second or third) and he now has a good job, or his own business, or his own church, but the question of success is never really settled. The Macho Man must ask himself continually, "Am I really a success as a man?"

Insecurity is the culprit. Until a man hears an *authorized* father-figure in his life say, "Well done," he will never really know if he is truly "O.K." Until some man that really matters to him says, "You're doing a good job; keep up the good work!," he never really knows where he stands in life. That demon of insecurity has come to live in his soul, and only another man—a "father"—can get it out.

Some Macho Men are former Wimps who grew tired of the emptiness of the approval of women. They may have wandered longingly back out to the porch several times before finally striking out on their own. They may even try Macho, then Wimp, then Macho again. Neither will satisfy.

In the great tradition of our many cultural icons of machismo—John Wayne, Clint Eastwood, and Sylvester Stallone—the Macho Man appears attracted to clothing that attempts to broadcast a message to other men: "Hey guys, I am a real man, you know. Can't you tell by how rugged my clothes look?" Like the Wimp, he seeks the affirmation he so desperately needs, but he is looking for it in the wrong place.

Typically, it is easier to recognize the Macho Man more by what he does than what he wears. After sharing with a group of men at a retreat once, a young man came up to me and declared with seeming boldness that he had never had a father but that that did not matter because God had become his father. "I'm one of the exceptions to the process," he told me. His body language and mannerisms, though, spoke another message. I watched him have great difficulty holding eye contact, and he held his upper body awkwardly stiff as if ready to attack or defend something. His jaw stayed clenched as he waited desperately for my approval of his challenging comments. Everything about his being spoke of tension and the need to be affirmed. I felt like jokingly saying (but didn't), "If God is your father, my friend, then it looks as if He's not doing a very good job!"

The Pitiful Porch-sitter

Apparently some men find themselves alone on the porch and simply decide to "have a seat." They neither retreat to the world of female dominance nor do they ambitiously set off on their own. They just park themselves and wait.

The Body of Christ is filled with *Porch-sitters*, men who are "saved" but not going anywhere in a hurry. Maybe they joined Christ's "club" because they were searching for relief from the father-wound and thought the church could help. Or maybe someone came by the porch and told them that joining the church would not necessarily require them to get up and do anything anyway, so they joined up from where they sat.

Many of these men entered Christendom during the every-head-bowed-and-every-eye-closed altar call routine. No sacrifice required, no courage needed, just sneak down to the altar here and "we'll get you saved." In my assessment many Wimps and cowardly Porch-sitters enter during these times of timid convert-making. (And we wonder why the men of the church sit idly by while the culture is literally going to hell.)

I think the Porch-sitter is less likely to dress effeminately or macho-like; he is more likely to dress in a boring manner. Because he wrestles with the same insecurities that plague the Wimp and the Macho, he apparently does not want to draw too much attention to himself. Feeling unsure about what to do, and not willing to take the other two extreme paths, he is left with no alternative but to wait and see what comes along. He may occasionally wander from the porch a bit but not for very long because his security is in staying in a familiar place, such as a long-standing job or a steady relationship.

Wimps, Machos, and Porch-sitters fill our modern world of men; they are literally everywhere. Some men travel between these three realms in great confusion and despair. Some days they seek the rule and approval of women; other days they seek it from men; still other days they hang out on the porch alone.

In any case these three types of men are not entering into manhood very well because the father appointed to meet them at the porch and take them into the fields of manhood never arrived, or he showed up but did a lousy job. For these men the Journey to Manhood has become derailed, the idea of connecting with Dad a forgotten dream. For these men the vision of living at the "right hand of authority" has perished. As far as these men are concerned, there is no king. If there ever was a king, he must be dead.

Has the King Died?

Men who have traveled these three paths come to believe that there is no King. The second plateau of authority they were designed to find and then master, that of the earthly father, has not been reached and crossed. Consequently, they have become hampered in their ability to move on in the journey toward the King of the Universe. They do not believe in the faithfulness of the earthly father, let alone a heavenly one. They have trouble trusting any man who is older than they (father-like figures) because they assume these older men must be like their dads. How can they trust God the Father whom they have never even seen when they cannot trust the father they can see?

These men live lives distant from the Father in heaven, and yet they spend their lives unwittingly searching for Him. That is to say, they keep trying to get back on the path. The fact that they are prone to seek approval from a father figure is the sign that God has designed them to complete the course. It seems, by about the age thirty, that the spirit of a man is old enough to realize that there is a King above all. Even so, many men never reach this King because their souls are too wounded and immature to enter into His presence. Emotionally, they are still little boys wishing for their Daddy. Until they deal with Dad, they are not going to finish the journey and find the King they so desperately seek. What a reprehensible place to live!

The enemy is there, of course, trying to ensure that they never find their way again. The devil knows that if lost men ever complete the Journey to Manhood and discover their destiny in the Father's chambers, his kingdom of darkness would start to fall under the resulting assault.

Even so we all carry a type of internal Father-focused compass in that each of us cry, "Abba! Father!" (Gal. 4:6). Like a laser-guided missile, this unconscious heart-cry draws us towards the Father, leaving us dissatisfied with anything less. Like Philip we longingly say, "Lord, show us the Father, and it is enough for us" (John 14:8).

Bly speaks of this drawing toward Kingly reality even though he is not a Christian. He notes,

> There is a King in the imaginative or invisible world.
> We don't know how he got there . . . At any rate, there
> is a King in sacred space.[8]

Recognizing that Bly and the other leaders of the emerging men's movement deny the Christian perspective of this King, it is nonetheless important to note that they openly acknowledge His existence. They recognize that men are searching for Him and searching hard. This seeking-yet-never-finding phenomenon may also explain why some men experience a so-called "mid-life crisis" in their mid-thirties to early-forties. They go through the Man's Man to King's Man transitional membrane and begin to fall into an empty chasm on the other side. Either their view of reality has no King or they are too father-wounded to believe in His existence.

To the men of our day, it appears as if there is no King. Or, if there is a King, He has died. At any rate, they do not see a way to reach Him.

Conclusion: We Are Men of Destiny

Until a man meets the heavenly Father, he cannot know what it is he was created to do. He will wander through his life like the Lost Boys of Peter Pan's Never Never Land. To be without a father is to be lost. Yet to be without the heavenly Father is to be lost forever.

Many men are lost in this life, even if they consider themselves Christians. In speaking to men at Christian retreats and seminars, I have noticed that most are not sure of what it is they were created to do. They are "wandering for Jesus." Yes, they usually know the basics of Christian manhood, but few seem to know what their specific task in life really is.

This Lost Boy syndrome is also true of the men outside of the church. A Kingdom Man must reach and enter the King's chamber and get his marching orders directly from the Father.

As a good Son, Jesus declared, "Truly, truly, I say to you, the Son can do nothing of Himself, unless it is something He sees the Father doing; for whatever the Father does, these things the Son does in like manner" (John 5:19).

What would our nation look like if several hundred thousand men entered into the type of intimate father-son relationship that Jesus had with His Father wherein He discovered the very steps He was to take in His ministry? What untapped spiritual force would the church in the Western Hemisphere uncover were its men ever to walk in the Father-closeness in which Jesus walked? What amount of irreparable damage would we see inflicted upon the strongholds of Satan in America were we men to discover our destiny as Kingdom Men? What are the possibilities?

God willing, we are going to find out.

4.

Accepting the Call to Sonship

And I will be a father to you, and you shall be sons and daughters to Me, says the LORD almighty.

2 Corinthians 6:18

God is not looking for Christian men; He is looking for sons.

For most men in our day though, this will be a difficult message to hear because many of us are foreigners to the uncharted world of sonship. Most of us have never visited this place, let alone lived there long enough to know our way around.

When we were stranded on the porch in childhood, we were left to choose another path in life, something other than sonship. The counterfeit models of the Macho Man, Wimp, and Porch-sitter are variations on the theme of sonship rejection. To the degree that we have naively chosen one or more of these paths, we have chosen to reject the high calling of sonship.

In America most of us expend our energies on ourselves, and we think of this as "natural." Who would ever consider working for another man's success, never getting any credit or obvious reward for it? Who would, for the sake of another man, be willing to endure hard labor for, say, eight or ten years in a line of work that was different than that of his anticipated occupation? Who would ever give up his own personal identity, his fame, in order to promote the name and reputation of another man? Who in his right mind would do such seemingly foolish things? A son.

The Call to True Greatness

The nation we live in is filled with great men—great in stature, great in thought, and great in deed. Certainly many of these virile giants have proven capable of accomplishing tremendous works, some in the name of humanism, some in the name of false gods, and some in the name of Jesus.

We often see these incredible deeds, or these incredible men, and we place much emphasis on the apparent greatness of it all. Like the prophet Samuel, we often look at the exterior, whereas God looks at the heart (1 Sam. 16:7). In this regard, the Bible teaches that the Father is not looking for great men as we count greatness.

What then is the Father looking for in men, if not earthly greatness?

Observing the lives of King Saul and his successor David, we get a glimpse at what the Father is truly seeking in men. The Scriptures reveal that one was a son, the other just a great king.

King Saul pursued his personal agenda to his own demise. What disqualified King Saul, more than anything else, was that he failed to seek after God's heart as a son would. The words of Samuel the prophet:

> But now your kingdom shall not endure. The LORD has
> sought out for himself *a man after His own heart,* and the
> LORD has appointed him as ruler over His people, be-
> cause you have not kept what the LORD commanded you
> (1 Sam. 13:14; emphasis added).

Saul was a great king, but the Father was not looking for
this type of greatness; He was looking for a man after His own
heart.

It was said of David that he was a man after God's own
heart (1 Sam. 13:14; Acts 13:22). Another way of saying this is
that he pursued God's will before his own. He made his heart's
desires and passions subservient to the wishes and plans of
God. He refused to pursue his own agenda, and though he
knew he was to be king, he waited patiently for God to exalt
him.

Ironically, Saul himself eventually realized this truth and
acknowledged that God was seeking for a man with the heart
of a son. In a jealous rage, Saul set out to pursue David with
an army of three thousand men, and at one point in the
search, he turned aside into a cave to relieve himself, unaware
that the outhouse he had chosen was the very place where
David and his rag-tag band of men were hiding. Here, David
had the opportunity to take Saul's life and become king, but
instead he stealthily cut off a piece of Saul's coat before Saul
left the cave. As Saul was walking away, David called out to him
and showed him the edge of his robe as the sign that he could
have killed him but did not.

When David put Saul's life and well-being before his very
own, he became like a son to Saul, or we could say he expressed *sonship* toward the king. In doing so David ran a high
risk because Saul could have turned and had him killed. But
the gamble paid off. Note Saul's moving lament after David
spared his life this first time:

> Now it came about when David had finished speaking
> these words to Saul, that Saul said, "Is this your voice, *my
> son* David?" Then Saul lifted up his voice and wept. (1 Sam.
> 24: 16; emphasis added).

Forced in agony of soul to recognize the son-likeness of
David's noble deed, he addressed him as "my son." To under-

stand this fully, we must back up and consider some of the
words that David spoke to the king in this setting:

> And David said to Saul, "Why do you listen to the words
> of men, saying, 'Behold, David seeks to harm you'? Behold,
> this day your eyes have seen that the LORD had given you
> today into my hand in the cave, and some said to kill you,
> but my eye had pity on you; and I said, 'I will not stretch
> out my hand against my lord, for he is the LORD's
> anointed.' Now, *my father*, see! Indeed, see the edge of
> your robe in my hand" (1 Sam. 24:9-11a; emphasis mine).

Aha! There it is—the "my father"—spoken only as a true
son could. You see, in David's heart, he honored Saul not only
as his earthly leader and royal mentor but also as a father. Is
there any doubt as to why David could not bring himself to kill
King Saul? Who could kill his own father, no matter how evil
he had become?

Nevertheless, Saul soon forgets David's childlike innocence
and how he spared his life; Saul seeks to kill David again. Once
more God delivers the falling king into David's trustworthy
hands, only this time David steals Saul's spear and the water
jug next to his head as he sleeps. After moving a safe distance
away, David calls out to those who were supposed to be watching the king and derides them for their inability to protect
him.

Saul's solemn remarks reveal the degree to which David's
sonship proved to be a mightier force than the world's finest
army. Worldly greatness had fallen at the feet of spiritual
sonship. A selection of Saul's familial comments:

> Then Saul recognized David's voice and said, "Is this your
> voice, *my son* David? . . . I have sinned. Return *my son*
> David, for I will not harm you again because my life was
> precious in your sight this day. . . . Blessed are you, *my son*
> David; you will both accomplish much and surely prevail (1
> Sam. 26:17,21,25; emphasis mine).

Because of David's aggressive acts of sonship, Saul was
forced to return the familial exchange with "my son." The
greatest leader the nation could supply was powerless to resist
the overwhelming truth that God was choosing a son over him
to be king. Human greatness had failed; sonship had conquered.

Years later, when the time came to find David's replacement, did the Father relax His standards and pursue a great man to become king? No, He wanted someone who knew sonship and who could be His son. Of this future king, the prophet Nathan said,

> When your days are complete and you lie down with your fathers, I will raise up your descendant after you, who will come forth from you, and I will establish his kingdom. He shall build a house for My name, and I will establish the throne of His kingdom forever. I will be a *Father* to him and he will be a *son* to Me . . . (2 Sam. 12:7- 14a; emphasis mine).

Historically, Nathan speaks of King Solomon, David's earthly son, but prophetically he speaks of Jesus the King, God's heavenly Son.

One day every great man must learn that the Father is not seeking after human greatness; He is seeking after sons.

The Father Is Still Looking

The Father calls each of us to become sons, generically meaning sons *and* daughters. We are not called to be God's equal, nor his slaves, but His children. This special relationship denotes submission, but the child is not a slave. There is also the hint of the vesting of authority, but the child is not the Father's equal.

Our model, of course, is Jesus. He was and is the perfect Son. While on earth He demonstrated the kind of relationship the Father seeks from all of His children. As a son, Christ preoccupied Himself with the work and will of His Father (John 5:19). As a son He claimed that when He spoke He spoke only that which the Father had instructed Him (John 8:28). As a son, even when His desires conflicted with His Father's will, he chose the Father's way, not His own (Matt. 26:39). Though He was the most sacred and religious man to ever set foot on the earth, our Lord demonstrated that what the Father is truly after in men is not religious piety but sonship.

It is very hard for a father, whether an earthly father or the heavenly Father, to get things done without sons. Hirelings simply don't work out as well because they have no abiding commitment to the success of the father. The chief motivation of the earthly hireling is to get paid—to receive the material reward. In the same way, the chief motivation of the spiritual hireling is also to get paid—a free ticket to heaven. The Father, however, is not looking for hireling workers (Christians who sign up in order to go to heaven); He is only looking for sons.

Becoming spiritual sons is the fundamental means whereby men relate to God. As we have seen with King Saul and David, sonship is the only relationship the Father accepts and is therefore the one legitimate avenue for entrance into His Kingdom. The man who willingly approaches as a son will discover his destiny; he will find his life.

As the perfect Son, Jesus modeled the death-to-self attitude of true sonship. The emphasis of His teachings and of His life was not getting Himself or others "saved," as in "going to heaven" versus "going to hell." This was a given for all who would surrender their lives to the Father. Rather, Christ's emphasis was on being a faithful son (John 5:19) and inviting others to join Him as joint heirs (Rom. 8:16,17; Matt. 5:9; Luke 6:35). It is impossible, therefore, to embrace God or to reach Kingdom Manhood without embracing the call to sonship.

Even so, fatherless cultures progressively discard this idea. Why? We reject the heavenly Father because we reject the earthly father. As we reject earthly sonship, we reject heavenly sonship.

First the Natural

Can men who have been raised in a fatherless day recapture this special gift? Many leaders with whom I have talked are somewhat pessimistic about this, but the Bible gives great hope that receiving and embracing the call to sonship is not only possible in our cursed day but is fully expected. But the process may not be as spiritual as we might expect. In fact, the process is very natural.

For more than a hundred years, since the time of the Industrial Revolution, we men have been estranged from the work and life of the earthly father, and now as a culture, we are estranged from the work and life of the heavenly Father.

We are first called to sonship in the natural, then in the spiritual, because, as the apostle Paul taught, the natural must come first, then the spiritual (1 Cor. 15:46). The material world is our tutor for things of the spiritual world. If we miss sonship in this realm, we will miss it in the spiritual realm as well.

Jesus Himself was first called to earthly sonship (as Joseph's son), then to spiritual sonship (as the firstborn Son of God). Christ knew as early as age twelve that God was His real Father; nevertheless he submitted himself to an earthly father first (Luke 2:49-51). Incredibly, God in the form of a man submitted himself to His own developmental principle—first the natural, then the spiritual.

Because the father-son breakdown occurred first in the natural, it will be necessary to go back and repair it in the natural. Furthermore, until men receive natural fathering, they will almost certainly live out their lives emotionally distant from their heavenly Father no matter how "spiritual" they may appear on the outside. Tragically, this is the pitiful lot of many men in the Christian Church, including some of those we look to as pastors and spiritual leaders.

Men who try to circumvent their need for earthly fathering often wind up stuck at an emotional maturity ceiling that hampers them from hearing the Father's voice. Because they are unskilled at listening to Dad here below, they cannot hear their heavenly Father's personal instructions. And, as we have already seen, without an intimate relationship with the Father, Christian men can fall into a sort of wandering-for-Jesus Christianity.

Because many of us have been injured by the father-wound, we have come to protect our emotions very closely. I see men everywhere unwittingly clutching their pain like half-crazed paupers clinging to their last piece of bread. They do not want anyone touching their soul for fear he will stir up the pain or do even more damage to the wound. Their hurt is great, yet most have learned to simply live with it.

The question emerges: "Can the men of our day be healed?" Agony of the soul has become normal, so normal we hardly even notice it until someone comes along and starts poking around in the father-wound. It is time to start poking, though, because until we touch the father-wound and see it treated, we cannot go beyond it. We will live at the soul age of six or eight or twelve or whenever it was when Dad hurt us.

Outrageous as it may seem, the solution that the Bible suggests is quite uncomplicated: Fatherless men simply need . . . fathers. We must move ahead with caution, for we are about to embark upon a part of our journey for which many are not yet well-prepared. The next step in the Journey to Manhood will take us out of the comfortable realm in which most of us have lived our lives and thrust us into a whole new world of challenges and experiences. So before we discuss the serious notion of setting out to find a father, which is where we are headed, we need to ask ourselves a potentially disquieting question: "Am I ready to leave the kitchen?"

Out of the Kitchen, Boys

We do not realize just how dependent upon women we have become.

A sudden heart attack killed Barry's father when he was only ten. Before this time Barry remembers his dad mostly as a passive man. Mom and Grandma ruled the roost. In the years following his father's death, Barry went to church some and even spent a couple years at a Christian college, but he found himself becoming involved in pornography, illicit sex, and the occult.

Looking back Barry would characterize himself as a "seeker" during these years, but he was not quite sure what it was he was seeking. After all, he knew where God was and how to access Him. He also understood what the occult had to offer, and that did not hold his attention either.

Finally, Barry became an active member in a local church that had a discipleship program for men. Working with one of the ministers and a small group of other men, Barry began to see the powerful hold his mother still had on his life. He lived at home rent free. His mother provided him a car, gas money, and insurance. Mom even gave Barry spending money and did his laundry. He was totally dependent upon her, and he was not even aware of it.

Barry drew his identity from his mom. His source of encouragement and support was maternal. Even after Barry got married, he would still run home several times each week for advice or a free meal. When he was not leaning on his mother for support, he would lean on his wife Cathy.

Barry was trapped by his own unwillingness to break away from the overpowering influence of the women in his life. Like the pitiful Wimp, he could not bring himself to cut the apron strings and get out of the kitchen, even though he knew this was essential for his development as a man.

On the Road to Thebes

Why was Barry so powerless to move away from his dependence on women by himself? Many modern psychologists believe that little boys fall in love with their mothers in what Freud referred to as the Oedipus, or Oedipal, complex. Understanding this curious developmental phenomenon may lend some insight into what adult men go through in leaving the kitchen.

In their marvelous work, *The Father Book: An Instruction Manual*, three respected experts from the Minirth-Meier Clinic attempt to simplify this strange occurrence for us:

> Then, there is that Oedipal complex everyone hears about. It occurs with boys at about three years of age and will deeply influence their whole lives. We think it works about this way. The small boy, just now getting a handle on this man-woman business, falls in love with Mommy. It's certainly not a sexual attraction of the sort we usually associate with "falling in love." It is at once much more naive and much more profound than that. Daddy becomes a dangerous rival. The lad may push Daddy away from Mommy, or insinuate himself between them. He will demand Mommy's full attention, drawing her away from the rival. When he grows up, he will marry Mommy. Then a curious, subtle shift happens. He observes that the bond between Mommy and Daddy is a strong one. They are well wedded to each other. He cannot marry Mommy. Rather, he will marry a lady like Mommy. In the child's heart, the relationships in this family fall gracefully into line. Mommy is Mommy, wed to Daddy who is Daddy, and the child is free to be a little child. The child has no emotional responsibility save to be loved and to grow. It is a very liberating realization.[1]

The Oedipal complex derives its name from the Greek figure, King Oedipus. As an infant Oedipus was wounded in his feet (*oedipus* means "swollen foot") and left to die by his mother. His father, King Laiös of Thebes, had received an oracle that this son would grow up to kill him and ordered him killed, but his mother could not bring herself to allow this. The abandoned child was found and raised by another king. Later, Oedipus, hearing of the oracle and believing the parents who raised him were his own, flees his "homeland" and returns to Thebes. On the way there, he meets a man with whom he quarrels. In his anger Oedipus kills the man. Oedipus eventually arrives in Thebes, saves the people from a devastating plague, is crowned king, and marries the widowed queen, Iokastê. Some time later he discovers that the man he had killed was his own father and the woman he has married is his own mother. Horrified by this and by the curse his murder of the great king has brought on Thebes, he blinds himself and banishes himself until his death.

Truth can be found in the strangest of places, and I suspect this ancient myth is one of those places.

Like Oedipus it seems that we all wish we could marry our mothers, and unless something sturdy stands in the way, something we cannot kill, we will likely do just that. That something is supposed to be our fathers who confronts us on the road to Thebes. As the co-authors of *The Father Book* explain so poignantly, the son needs to see the unshakable reality that his father and mother are "well wedded to each other." At some point, the authors note, the son must realize "he cannot marry Mommy."

This is the emotional place every man must reach before he can continue on the path. Listen to the freeing finality of that last statement: "He cannot marry Mommy." Liberation only comes when a man finally realizes there is no opportunity to remain dependent on the mother figure in his life. This forceful idea sets the boy free to "love and to grow." He is no longer bound by the maternal power of his mother. He is set free to move forward in his Journey toward Manhood.

But what if the father is absent, or is so weak that the son can "kill" him on his way to Thebes—that place where Mom is

Queen? The metaphor here is powerful. In the end, we find that killing our father and marrying our mother brings a curse, blindness, and banishment.

This sounds very much like our modern situation to me.

A Second Postpartum

In his new book, *Father and Son*, Gordon Dalbey deals at length with this issue of breaking away from the mother, devoting an entire chapter to what he calls, "Cutting the Cord: A Second Postpartum." Here he says that

> . . . a second postpartum looms—equally momentous for the male child and painful for the mother—in which the male child must move from being mother's boy to being father's son.[2]

There are two vital factors about this maternal severing, what one author refers to as, "Saying good-bye to WOMAN," that must be underscored here, and both of these have to do with the role of the father.

First, it is important to point out that a man does not reach Kingdom Manhood simply by breaking away from the mother figures in his life. As we laid out in chapter 3, the sojourning boy on his way to Kingdom Manhood desperately needs another tutor, one appropriate for the next leg of the journey. Whether the "boy" is five or thirty-five makes no difference; this next step is essential.

About this Dalbey comments:

> One does not become a man simply by rejecting and breaking from his mother. The larger masculine—the father and the community of men—must be reckoned with, hearkened unto as well. Otherwise, an edge of resentment, even hostility, remains and focuses eventually on women. Because the mother is present and accessible, the boy's most focused emotion says, "Let go of me, Mom!" But, his more primal cry is rather, "Come and get me, Dad!"[3]

Otherwise, we have a young boy standing on the porch alone. This says, then, that the man, who is saying good-bye to WOMAN, must also say hello to MAN.

There is also a second pivotal issue here that tells of the need for a father figure. A young man is not capable of making the break on his own, even if he wants to be. There must be another man, namely a father, to help the son make the transition.

All of this is not to say that a man's lack of sonship is his father's fault—it most definitely is not. The father may have slowed the boy down, but he cannot stop the boy from embracing the call to sonship. Nevertheless, before a boy will take that leap away from Mom, he will need the help and encouragement of a father, one who keeps saying, "Come on, you can do it!"

Reaching the Other Tree

A few years back, a group of us spent a day on a professional "ropes course" at a nearby college. Like a mini-boot camp experience, the course is designed to teach people trust and teamwork and help them discover some of their gifts. Different physical and mental obstacles are set up in the woods to challenge the trainees to use their bodies and their minds and to pull together as a team. We had failed at the Lava Pit, and the Low Cable Walk, but we were successful in scaling the Wall—the fourteen-foot wall, that is—and now we were facing our last and most challenging obstacle of the day: the Cable Walk.

There we stood, staring at a thirty-foot length of steel cable that was tightly suspended between two trees at more than twenty feet in the air. One of the instructors said, all too casually, "The object of this event is to climb the tree, walk the length of the cable, turn around and walk back."

Two more cables spanned the trees and were positioned directly above the first cable at just the right height to hold onto. The catch, though, was that these upper cables crisscrossed the walking cable, so as one edged toward the center, where they were bolted to the walking cable and just where these upper cables were needed the most, they were at about the height of one's ankles.

"You'll be wearing a safety harness that will be connected to another cable above you," one instructor informed us, "and this will catch you in the event that you fall."

I am sure we were all supposed to be comforted by this added piece of information, but judging by the looks on most of the faces around me, I suspected the others were as skeptical as I was.

"Finally," the other instructor added, "we would encourage you to attempt the walk blindfolded!"

As I climbed the tree pegs that made a ladder up to the cable, blindfold already in place, I wondered, "Why am I doing this?" Though I was never able to fully answer the question, I pushed on just the same. As I left the safety of one tree, a compelling conviction ran through my mind: "If I can just reach the other tree, I'll be a success."

Some time later I realized that in the life of a fatherless man, a father figure is the other tree!

The Journey to Manhood will require that men cut the cords of emotional maternal dependence that have been in place since birth. Men will need to gently but firmly move away from the soul power that is held over them, sometimes unwittingly and sometimes purposefully, by women. To go forward men will need to move out of the kitchen of their souls and toward the porch.

Conclusion: The Father Is Looking for a Few Good Sons

Of all the ideas I am attempting to convey in this book, the call to sonship is perhaps the most radical and challenging. Accepting sonship, conceptually, is no big deal; the biblical case for approaching God as a son is not a difficult one to make. The rub comes with embracing the process of moving into sonship. Accepting the training and faithful ministry of another man, one who becomes like a father to you, is much more difficult than simply accepting the abstract idea. We are talking about a complete 180-degree shift for many men.

In essence the call to sonship is at the very heart of my message. Miss this, and this book becomes another superficial self-help book for men, only with a Christian slant. Certainly, this is not my desire.

On the other hand, if a man will embrace the call to sonship and all that goes with it, he will move into a new understanding of his relationship with God. He will move forward toward discovering his destiny, toward a deeper understanding of his purpose, toward the unshakable strength of mature manhood. He will move forward toward the mission that the Father has for the men of this generation. And he will move forward toward a deeper relationship with his wife, children, and others. In every way, on every front, on both spiritual and natural levels, the man who embraces the call to sonship, and is also willing to accept the natural process of becoming a son, will advance into a whole new era in his life.

We would do well to remind ourselves that when God the Father had an important job to do on the earth, He did not send a "great" man—like Saul or Hitler—He sent His Son. Today, the Father still has important work to do on the earth, and He is even now looking for sons to do the job.

5.

Finding a Father

For if you were to have countless tutors in Christ, yet you would not have many fathers; for in Christ Jesus I became your father through the gospel.

(1 Corinthians 4:15)

A funny scene from the movie *Hook* portrays a poignant message that father-wounded men truly need to understand.

Hook and the pirates are trying to brainwash Peter Pan's son, Jack, into thinking that Hook is his real father and that Peter was a bad father. The pirates, who are comically inept at everything they attempt, have set up a mock baseball stadium for Jack to hit the home run he never could because his busy father never came to his games.

Some of the goofy pirates are holding placards in the grand stands that are supposed to say, "Home Run Jack." Instead they are switched around and in fact read, "Run Home Jack." The easily excitable pirate crowd begins to chant, "Run home, Jack! Run home, Jack! Run home, Jack!", and before Hook has a chance to intervene and get the placards switched back, the words penetrate Jack's heart. For a brief moment, he is confronted with the interior call to return home to his father. I would call this "returning to the porch."

Like Jack the men of our day have been "kidnapped" by an evil world system that presents the putrid lie that fathers are evil and not really needed. Like Jack these men have been wounded and left with a weakened will. And like Jack we could use some air-head pirates right about now who unwittingly hold the placards incorrectly.

Run Home, Jack!

Though it might sound a bit odd to say so here, every man will eventually discover that he cannot get manhood from a book. For that matter, he cannot get it from a seminar, or even a men's retreat. Although he can learn *about* manhood through these mediums, a man can only *get* manhood from someone who has it and is willing to take the time to share it, namely another man. Anyone who tries to tell you otherwise is probably trying to sell you something (like a book or a seminar). More specifically, the only kind of man who can show us the way to sonship is a father. This is one who has been to the Father before and can lead us there. If we are to find *the* Father, we will need the help of *a* father. Like Jack we will need to "run home."

Not everyone is willing to hear this, of course. The Macho Man, in all his humanistic wisdom, cannot fathom the idea that he may need another person to help him. He still believes he can get to manhood on his own. The Wimp, in all his Victorian vigilance, may be much too comfortable living in the world of mothers to be at all interested in where we are headed—the world of fathers. And the Porch-sitter, in his sheer fear and idleness, may be too paralyzed to move off the porch at all.

Nevertheless, for those who have languished in these miserable pursuits long enough to be desperate, I invite you to run with me back home—back to the porch—and give sonship another shot.

Mentor or Father?

Before moving into the practical aspects of searching for a father, it would be helpful to pause briefly here to make a distinction between what I am referring to as a father and what some are calling mentors. Because the concept of mentoring is receiving renewed attention these days, thanks primarily to the secular men's movement, it is all the more essential that we differentiate between the two terms. Both mentors and fathers are needed in our day, but they do not necessarily serve the same function.

For purposes of our discussion, a mentor could be described as a specialized trainer who helps the understudy in a particular area of life. He is like the tutors Paul speaks of in 1 Corinthians 4:15, where he differentiates between teachers and the one who would be a father to the people.

A father, though he may do some mentoring within the overall scope of his work with the son, is one who carries a more comprehensive burden for the man's complete development versus his specialized development. The understudy is not just a student; he is his son. This denotes a broader scope of ministry and a more personal relationship than that of the mentor and his student.

In his outstanding book, *The Fine Art of Mentoring*, Ted Engstrom has attempted to outline the essential attributes of the mentor. He holds that there are six basic characteristics:

Generally speaking, a mentor

- is a person who has achieved superior rank on an organizational or professional ladder;
- is an authority in his field as the result of disciplined work, study, and experience;
- has a certain measure of influence in his chosen field;
- is genuinely interested in a protégé's growth and development; and
- is willing to commit time and emotional energy to a relationship with an understudy. This goes beyond mere

interest and is commitment that, more often than not, is intense.[1]

In short the mentor is a specialist in a given field who is willing to pass on his knowledge and skill in a personal way to an apprentice. On the other hand, the father figure may not be an expert in any given field. His qualifications come more from his fathering skills, his ethical foundations, and his over-all spiritual maturity than from his technical, vocational knowledge.

Looking at the ministry the Apostle Paul had with men like Timothy as a possible model, one might conclude that a father would be a man who

- is willing to bring the son before the throne of God on a regular basis;
- is willing and able to give spiritual oversight to the son and hold him accountable for his actions;
- cares for the son with the depth of love normally associated with biological children;
- is willing to invest significant time and resources in the comprehensive (versus specialized) development of the son, touching the body, soul, and spirit in his fatherly ministry;
- genuinely demonstrates the life and character of the heavenly Father;
- is willing to share his work with the son as a key training environment; and
- imparts his worldview to the son in the course of work and play.

Generally speaking, the ministry of a father precedes that of the tutor in terms of the natural development of a man. During the younger years of a man's life, he does not need the specialized training of a machinist or a carpenter; he needs the paternal training of a father. Once the more fundamental work of the father is completed, and the young man has built a solid foundation in his life, he will then head off to college, or into the working world. It is at this point that he would normally need a mentor.

In our situation, of course, a man may very well need both a father and a mentor at the same time. At one point in my own journey, there were actually four men working on me—a father figure and three mentors. Each of the mentors played specialized and needed roles in my life, but only one man played the role of a father. Though each of the mentors had a measure of fatherliness about his tutoring, which is essential to all biblical male leadership (see chapter 9), only one of these men actually held the level of accountability for me that accompanies fathering.

We will likely have many tutors or mentors available to us in life. Still, I think it may be difficult to replace the work and ministry of a father figure. If you have never had a father, or if your experience with your biological dad was less than ideal, I invite you to give it another shot—go find a man who will hold you in his heart before the throne. Overcome your fear and take that first step.

The following are meant to be guidelines for the courageous.

Recognize the Phase You Are In

The most masculine thing that any man can do in these fatherless times is to be honest with himself and others about where he is *not*. It takes a real man to admit that he has yet to arrive at, or in many cases, even come close to becoming a King's Man. When a man is willing to honestly assess his location on the journey to manhood, he is in a good place, even if he is still a Mama's Boy, for now he can sight his goal and discern what needs to be done to reach that goal. This man will be motivated to move forward.

Where Are You?

A great many of us think we are farther down the path than we are. Too often a Mama's Boy, Daddy's Boy, or Man's Man will think of himself as having reached Christian manhood simply because he walks in some semblance of a relationship with God and is not into any "heavy" sin. His wife and others are not on his case about becoming a Kingdom Man, and he was just recently elected to be a church deacon or elder. He may think, "What's the big deal? I'm doing all right."

This kind of man sees the phenomenally tight relationship Jesus had with the Father and knows he does not have that level of intimacy but chalks it up to the Jesus-could-do-it-be-cause-He-was-God rationale and summarily dismisses any thought of ever pressing into the King's throne room himself. He thinks, in other words, "I can't have that quality of relation-ship with the Father—I'm just a man!" Without a better per-spective, he may assume his masculine standing with God is normal, even advanced. After all, he lives in a day of Wimps, Machos, and Porch-sitters, and by these comparisons, he is doing great! But in God's eyes, is he normal?

What Is Normal for a Kingdom Man?

If a man is not spending significant time in daily intimate interaction with the Father, if he has not yet spent the years needed in each of the three previous phases to develop his character and stature, and if he has not yet discovered his destiny in the way Jesus did, knowing who He was and what He was called to do, then he has not yet reached Kingdom Manhood! He may be a great Man's Man, in that he has mastered the many dimensions of Christian virility needed to function well in this life. Even so, unless he has discovered his Kingdom vocation in a relationship with his Father, like Jesus did, to Whose image God is trying to conform us all (Rom. 8:29), then he has fallen short of the goal of true manhood set before him—he has not yet become a King's Man.

The first step for the aspiring Kingdom Man is the hard-ball assessment. I trust this book will help you in taking that first step.

Seek a Father, Not a Teacher

Back on the porch now, it is time to begin pursuing a father again.

When we were young, we were unable to comprehend what was happening to us as the curse of the fatherless played itself out in our families. But we are older now, and in this place of our lives we can understand and we can take action. *Then* we were not responsible for our fatherless condition, but *now* we are. If you have read this far in this book, you can no longer say, I did not know that God could more than make up for what Satan stole from me in my younger days. You are now accountable to be trained as a Kingdom Man—to seek a father.

Timothy Found One

In a day when few of us trust other men, especially older men, it becomes difficult to believe that another man may have something we desperately need. The re-fathering we crave (whether consciously or unconsciously) cannot come from our children or our wives, and though God could give it to us directly, He has chosen not to. Rather, He uses the men of the church as His earthly vessels, filled up with His Fatherly heart to be poured out on other men.

The apostle Paul was one such father. In his letter to the Corinthian church, he speaks about his relationship to the believers there and notes in particular the ministry of one of his "sons," Timothy (1 Cor. 4:15-17). Why would Paul refer to Timothy as a child or son (see 2 Tim. 1:2)? Was Timothy's fathering background less than adequate so that he would now need a father? The Bible tells us that Timothy's mother and grandmother were righteous women (2 Tim. 1:5) but that his "father was a Greek" (Acts 16:1) and apparently not a believer. Paul's emphasis on Timothy's righteous maternal background and his contrast between Timothy's Jewish and believing mother and his "Greek" father may lead the reader to wonder if something may have been lacking in Timothy's fathering experience. After all, the curse of the fatherless was as prevalent in Roman culture as it is in Western society today. At any rate, Paul embraced Timothy as his "son in the Lord."

I am convinced that Paul may have been seeing something strategic that we need to see today. In both his letters to Timothy, the great apostle consistently refers to him as a "beloved son" or "child." (The same held true for his letter to Titus.) At first, this show of verbal affection may be taken as only spiritual in nature because we often hear Christians refer to other believers as brothers or sisters in Christ. Sometimes this is with sincerity and understanding; sometimes this is just "Christianese."

Nevertheless, as one begins to examine the functional father-son type of relationships Paul had with Timothy, one begins to see something much deeper than a Christian cliché. A telling sign of the nature of their relationship was that Paul allowed Timothy the privilege of working with him in his ministry (Acts 16:3). Historically, this has been the forum where fathers trained their sons. In the work environment, a man's spirit is revealed, for good or for bad, and it is this spirit of a father that the son needs to see and absorb.

Paul also trusted Timothy to accurately represent him to other believers (1 Cor. 4:17) and to support him in his work with other cities (1 Thess. 3:2). Again, though it is certainly possible to have a paid worker represent you to others, the most accurate and authoritative representation of a father is always his son.

More than once this great apostle was willing to share his growing fame with Timothy, often opening his letters with references to Timothy in the salutations (2 Cor. 1:1; Phil. 1:1; Col. 1:1; 1 Thess. 1:1; Philem. 1). This honor was not extended to other associate ministers, only to the son who had served Paul faithfully.

Both Paul and Timothy seemed to recognize the need they had for each other, which is the way it should be between fathers and sons. The Bible says that Paul "wanted this man to go with him" (Acts 16:3). Timothy, for his part, responded by going and by consistently acting as a faithful son to Paul, even when others were seeking their own interests (Eph. 2:19-22). In fact, Timothy paid a painful price to become Paul's son, the Bible says that Paul decided to circumcise Timothy before taking him on the road with him (Acts 16:3). Timothy was committed!

In seeking to find a father, you may discover that you too have to "give up" something in order to embrace the call to sonship. Like Paul a father may ask you to change something about your lifestyle or appearance, something that simply makes life easier for him, not you. Paul apparently did not want to deal with the does-a-man-need-to-be-circumcised-to-be-a-Christian? issue every time he was with the Jews. It was simply easier to deal with the appearance issues at the outset.

We also see that the interaction between Paul and Timothy was not a casual Christian relationship or even simply a close ministry relationship. Paul's aggressive training coupled with Timothy's faithfulness and servant heart forged a father-son bond. Paul needed the allegiance and services of a true son, and Timothy needed the training and nurturing of a Kingdom father. Like an earthly surrogate standing in for the Father above, Paul developed Timothy's manhood in a way that only a father could and helped him reach his destiny in God. This great apostle understood that only a father could teach Timothy *sonship*.

Are You the Son of a Greek Father?

When Timothy joined Paul's apostolic team, he was the son of a Greek man. Timothy's earthly father begot him, but was he a true father to him? Would this man have developed Timothy's gifts and callings to the place where Timothy could emerge as the senior elder at the city of Ephesus? Not likely. Would this man have led Timothy to the foot of the Cross and then to the throne room of the ancient God of the Hebrews? I do not think so. Would this man have faithfully taught and instructed Timothy in the biblically defined ways of his heavenly Father? I would conclude not.

Today, we see many households with righteous mothers and "Greek" fathers. It does not take the boy growing up in these homes long to realize that religion is a woman's affair; it is not something men take seriously. Though a youngster might get dragged off to church by his mother and grandmother for years, he will likely leave the church as soon as he is old enough to "escape." This could have been the path that Timothy may have eventually taken.

Is this not the story of our modern situation? Not until a "Paul" comes along, someone who is willing to actually do the job the biological father refused to do (or was incapable of doing), will we see the fatherless men of our day begin to sit as elders in the city gates as Timothy eventually did. God is not caught short, then, when cultures become fatherless. He has provided for the re-fathering of the fatherless through the Kingdom Men of the Church. We desperately need these surrogate fathers to help us experience the sonship that we missed the first time around.

Certainly, the fathers, or more mature men of the Church, need to call out to the fatherless young men, and this is part of the message of this book. But the young men must also call out to the fathers. Men should not settle for the Greek fathering they have received. They should seek and embrace a father like unto the apostle Paul.

Today is the day, then, when men—men like you and me—need to make a solemn commitment before the living God, the Father in heaven, that we will not rest until we have found a father in the faith.

Look among Your Own People First

Many pastors will thank me for adding these next few paragraphs.

Before a man runs off to find a father-like man to train him in the ways of the Lord, he needs to be firmly reminded of the negative inference of that age-old adage—the grass is always greener on the other side of the fence.

Because I have been sharing this message with men for some time in seminars and retreat settings, I have some experience with how men are likely to respond to what they read in these pages. A man who takes an assessment of his location on the Journey to Manhood may become desperate for a father in his life, and this is good. This deep sense of personal need will become the emotional fuel that carries the man through the days of hard searching ahead. But processing raw desperation can also lead some men to impulsive action. One of the impetuous moves that I have observed is that men will sometimes take a quick look around them in the local church and conclude that there is no one there who can do the job. Because the man looking to be discipled is all too aware of the faults and shortcomings of the men around him, and because he is unskilled at recognizing true fatherhood in other men, he quickly concludes, "I must go elsewhere to find a father!"

In these situations men often forget that Paul was human, too. Because of the abundance of revelation that he carried, we sometimes think of him as saint-like or near perfect. But Paul likely had many of the same problems the men in our local church have, possibly a lack of compassion, excessive pride, or impatience. Because of the infirmity that he bore in his flesh (2 Cor. 12:7), which may have been a partial blinding or crippling, he may not have looked like a real Man's Man or some super father at first glance. He may have looked rather plain, maybe even a little feeble.

Because of this I would caution men to move carefully with the power of this message. Before making any decisions, please finish the book; make sure you have the whole picture. Also, the final chapter gives some practical "next steps" advice that you will want to consider before deciding upon a course of action.

Once you have made a commitment to fostering sonship in your life, begin to seek a father among your own people first. Talk to your pastor about what you are seeing and thinking and get his input and counsel. Ask him to recommend some men in your local church whom he might consider capable and potentially willing to develop a relationship with you. Meet and talk with these men about the needs you are sensing for a father figure in your life. Encourage them to read this book and suggest they attend one of my seminars to get a better handle on the message themselves.

Only after a man has made a thorough and exhaustive search in the local church would I encourage him to seek elsewhere for the man or men that he will need to help him in his journey.

Unfortunately, the reality is that many churches do not have a single Kingdom Man (let alone several) who could do for the young men what Paul did for Timothy. In other situations there may be a couple Kingdom Men, but they may already be consumed with other matters. In either case a man may need to look outside of his current fellowship, maybe even relocate. Both of these are radical ideas indeed, but we live in a desperate and fatherless hour. For some the steps of becoming a son in the natural will be radical. But let the radical steps be the last resort, not the first.

Keep Seeking

As the implications of the call to sonship sink into a man, he will begin to recognize that we are facing a situation where there are many more needy sons than there are Kingdom Men to father them. Clearly the Timothies outnumber the Pauls. A friend of mine says, "There are not many class A coaches available."

If leaving the kitchen and getting back to the porch seemed hard, wait until you begin looking for a father in the Lord in a day when Kingdom Fathers are in short supply. This is some of the hardest work that we may ever do in our lives. There may even be some major disappointments along the road. For instance, you may approach several men before finding one who is both willing and capable of extending this type of relationship to you. You may even start out with a man and step off the porch, as it were, only to find out later that he is really incapable of doing the job or that he has a different agenda in mind.

These and many other discouraging scenarios are very real, and it is possible that you will find yourself in a less than ideal situation as soon as you step out in this pursuit. Unless you are prepared for the likely setbacks, you may get blown out of the water with disenchantment. Only God's grace, coupled with your own unswerving tenacity, will see you through the process. I do not mean to overdramatize the situation, but I have seen many men start out in a sprint only to drop out before reaching the first turn. A man must ask the Father for His help and then set his face like flint and set his will to persevere.

Conclusion: Time to Swim Upstream

Returning to the porch and setting out to find a father—a father in the Lord—is hard work, but it is vital. It is the first step for most men in seeking out the Father in heaven. It is a recognition that there is a pathway to spiritual maturity and that the earthly father-figure is one of the key guides along the way.

Humanism preaches the independence and self-sufficiency of the individual. Christianity preaches the interdependence of the "Body of Christ" and complete sufficiency of God. To the degree that we "go with the flow" of our culture and reject the natural fathering ministry of the men God has appointed in our lives, we reject His abundant supply, and we embrace the self-destructive deceptions of our culture's false worldview.

Moreover, it is my conviction that *not* pursuing a father in the faith is the same as rejecting sonship. Drifting along lazily on the cultural currents with a wait-and-see attitude is more apt to take us further away from the goal of sonship than closer. Maybe it is time to start swimming upstream.

6.

Ruling the
Inner Kingdom

The Kingdom of God does not come with your careful observation, nor will people say, "Here it is," or "There it is," because the Kingdom of God is within you.

Luke 17:20, 21—NIV

At the root of our national leadership debacle is a deterioration in the ability of men to conduct *internal* government—to rule their own tripartite beings. For these men the body, soul, and spirit live, not in orderly harmony with each other as a result of being properly aligned, but in chaos. The inability of men to operate out of the developed strength of their internal will (spirit) has produced a generation of men ruled by their feelings (soul) and the flesh (body).

Rulers who lack this competence tend to breed chaos into that which they lead, whether it is a family, church, or city. No amount of leadership training can replace the essential leadership capability that is acquired when one learns to govern his internal being. If a man cannot rule himself, how can he effectively rule others? Societal law and order begins to break down at this point. For when a man has not been trained to or is not willing to, bring his body, soul, and spirit into order and submission, he will certainly not be submissive to others. If he tolerates anarchy in his inner being, he will produce anarchy in his exterior leadership. In this type of society, every man becomes a law unto himself. This, of course, is fast becoming the order of our day.

The impact of the Industrial Revolution and its role in the destruction of fatherhood cannot be fully understood until one looks at the long-range implications of the digression and disintegration of societies that lack self-government.

The Kingdom Man is called first and foremost to bring the rule of the Kingdom of God to his own life.

Self-Government

Self-government is the foundation for all societies as well as the prerequisite for true leaders. One who cannot lead himself is incapable of effectively leading others. Self-government could be described as the ability and choice to will oneself to do what one knows to be right. It is the voluntary governing of one's triune being under the Lordship of Christ. It is the free-will act of obedience to God's will as it is revealed to us in His Word. To know God's righteousness and refuse to do what He commands is sin (James 4:17). On the other hand, to know God's will and to be willing to act on it is self-government.

But How Does It Work?

Created in God's image, we are made up of three distinct dimensions—body, soul, and spirit (see diagram 1, p. 102). Put in simple terms, the *spirit* could be described as one's *will* or the place where a person decides what he will do. This should not be confused with one's passions—what we want to do. Rather, the will is the internal executive function vested with the authority and latent power to control one's behavior and thoughts. It is the seat of the conscience and the place of communion with the Spirit of God. The will (spirit) is the dimension that either obeys the voice of God or caves in to the impulses of the soul or the cravings of the flesh. It is the governing head of our three-part personhood. In its fallen state, the spirit of a man cannot effectively rule over the body and soul. Yet when a man's spirit is renewed in Christ, he receives the divine nature of God and can therefore begin to bring that redemption and order to his other two realms.

The soul is the origin of one's emotions, desires, or feelings such as anger, fear, and courage. The soul is where we feel. It is the home of our passions. This dimension gives us the ability to experience life, to have impressions. Though it is powerful, the soul was not designed to rule over a man's spirit. When the soul experiences fear, for instance, it advises the spirit to be cautious. The soul senses emotional pain and warns the spirit to back off from the situation. The soul senses success and encourages the spirit to celebrate. The soul is a separate yet integrated segment of our three-part personage. So, we see King David asking the Lord to speak to his soul as if it were a distinct entity, asking God to, "Say to my soul, 'I am your salvation'" (Ps. 35:3).

The third part of our being, the body, is the earthly vessel we currently live in. This dimension also senses conditions and sends messages to the spirit, but these conditions are of the material realm. The spirit takes these signals in and weighs them, taking action as it deems appropriate. With eating, for instance, the body experiences pleasure and says, "More, more, more!" The spirit must decide if more is appropriate and helpful. If not the spirit says, "Enough is enough." With exercise, the body encounters pain and says, "Stop!" The spirit must weigh the benefits of pressing through the pain and make the decision whether to stop or proceed. If more exercise is needed, the disciplined spirit says, "Keep going, we're not finished yet."

Like God Himself, there must be governmental order in the three parts of our being or else chaos will reign. Jokingly, I asked an audience once what would happen if God were to ever disagree with Himself (in His three parts, that is). Most laughed and said that was impossible. But is it? I reminded them of the time in the garden when Jesus prayed and asked for the cup of the cross to be removed if possible. Because he understood submission to the Father, Jesus quickly added that if His will was in tension with the Father's will, He wanted the Father's will to rule. How incredibly different history would be were it not for orderly government in the three dimensions of the God-head! The same holds true for us.

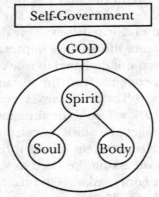

The Human Tripartite Being

Recognizing the Internal Coup D'état

Now that we see that inner order must be achieved by a right authority of the spirit over the body and soul of a person, we can begin to look at what happens when this order breaks down. The spirit of a man is designed to be the executive or leader of the three-part person, and the soul and body are supposed be submissive to it. These two realms can give *input* to, but never rule over, the spirit. If they usurp the authority of the spirit, the person experiences an *internal coup d'état*.

For instance, if a person's soul has overcome the authority and strength of his spirit, we would call this person "soulish" or emotionally unstable; he is controlled by his feelings. In our day the emotion that is most often out of control in men is rage. Many men are deeply angry at their fathers, at God, and at life, and they are unwilling and sometimes unable (at their present maturity level) to control this anger. Other feelings that sometimes spring from men's souls are fear, anxiety, loneliness, and greed. The man who allows these feelings to rule him is literally out of order, or out of control; rebellion has occurred on the most fundamental level. Orderliness has been lost internally. This is one type of interior coup d'état that can occur in the man who lacks self-government.

Other men are controlled by the third realm of their beings—the body. We would call this type of inner rebellion an *addiction*. Some of the more common of these might include addictions to sex, narcotics, alcohol, caffeine, sleep, and food. This type of man is controlled by these fleshly cravings and is captive therefore to his body. His spirit or will is not strong enough to rule over the powerful urges of the flesh, and so he is held prisoner to these seemingly invisible forces.

Some men, of course, are tossed to and fro between being controlled by both the soul *and* the body. If the spirit or will of a man is weak, or if he is unwilling to exercise its authority, it is not uncommon for him to be enslaved simultaneously by his two lesser realms. If the will cannot rule the emotions, it will likely not rule the flesh either.

Self-government then is the active process of ruling one's soul and body from the realm of the spirit and then submitting the spirit to the Father's will. This is the willingness and ability to lead one's self. If a person can be taught to govern his own triune being, he can probably learn to lead others. Without self-government, though, it is virtually impossible to lead anything else. You cannot export what you do not have.

The Challenge before Us

More than anything else, the lack of self-government in any society demonstrates the degree to which that society has rejected God's comprehensive right to rule over them. Astoundingly, most men in our day, including most Christian men, have never even heard of the term self-government, let alone been trained in it. Yet without self-government as a cultural foundation, society is destined to collapse under the weight of male lawlessness.

A Tale of Two Cities

Imagine a city where 70 to 80 percent of the men are biblically self-governed. These men have developed a heightened ability to manage their emotions and rule their bodies, and their well-developed spirits are submitted to the lordship of Christ. What would this city look like?

The male rage that reigns in so many other cities would nowhere be found. Violence, rape, and sexual assault would be virtually non-existent. The rate of suicide would be nil, as would the incidence of drunkenness and drug abuse. The home would be at peace, strife and racial tension seldom heard of. The workplace would be productive. The streets would be safe, and people not afraid. Laws would have been passed to reflect the godly values in these men's hearts, but it would not be the external government that restrained them; it would be their internal willingness and ability to be self-governed. The Kingdom of God is witnessed in the men and is therefore witnessed in the city.

Now let us look at another city. In this city 70 to 80 percent of the men lack biblical self-government. Nevertheless, because of the Christian consensus in days gone by, most of the civil laws are still biblically based. It is illegal, for instance, to get an abortion. Divorce is only allowed in instances of persistent sexual unfaithfulness and desertion. Restitution is required when a man steals from his neighbor, and so forth. What would this city look like?

The male rage is back, and it is not restrained by the civil laws. Because city ordinances prohibit public drunkenness, the jails are filled to overflowing. Racial tensions run high, and full-scale riots are frequent in spite of civil rights laws. Unrestrained men ignore divorce laws and simply leave their wives at will and illegally dally with other women whenever they please. Many of the laws are not even enforced because the police department and the courts are filled with corruption and bribe-takers. Whole sections of the city are given over to lawlessness as criminals, gangs, and drug dealers rule the streets. In time the righteous laws begin to be thrown out by unscrupulous legislators who care more about increasing their salaries (and the citizens' tax bills) and keeping their comfortable jobs than they do about justice in the city. Anarchy reigns everywhere, and the Kingdom is not visible.

It does not take a Ph.D. in sociology to figure out which city we would rather live in. But it does take some biblical wisdom to understand why the cities look so different. Like most modern politicians and civic leaders, many Christians have not discovered the true nature of real peace in their families and cities. Peace is not obtained through legislation (external controls), even if that legislation is godly; peace is obtained through biblical self-government (internal control). *Godly laws are not the cause of cultural reformation; they are the fruit of it.*

In the same way, the progressive passage of ungodly laws demonstrates the unwillingness of the people to be self-governed. One politician stated it well in a memo to his state legislature when arguing that the state's biblically based adultery statute should be overturned:

> While the presence of an adultery statute accomplishes nothing, it does have effects deleterious to respect for the law. Besides upholding the law to ridicule in the eyes of some, the existence of a statute *which seemingly will never be enforced* weakens the deterrent effect of the rest of the law . . . Now, community mores are such that retention of a law making adultery a crime does not seem justified.[1] (emphasis added)

The cities are not held together by their laws. The cities are cohesive relative to the willingness of the people, especially the leading men, to do the right thing. This is self-government; without it we are sunk.

Doing the Right Thing

I think it is no exaggeration to say that during the early part of the nineteenth century, the average man was more self-governed than most men in our day, including many men who declare themselves to be Christian. The rate of divorce was astoundingly low relative to today's figures, the work ethic was sturdy in a wholesale societal way, and the respect for women and children was much higher than in our increasingly barbaric 1990s. By and large, men were willing and able to hold themselves to a higher personal standard than they are in our day. We could say they had a stronger will.

But this willingness to do the right thing is nearly gone today. Men seem to live by their fleshly passions and soulish desires. Without a disciplined will, men are like ships without a rudder. No amount of Bible studies, prayer meetings, or Christian counseling will help the man whose volition is frail. More men's books and Christian retreats will be of little help either. These weak-willed men do not need more information; they need their wills strengthened. The question for these men is not "What is the right thing to do?" Rather, the question has become "How do I do the right thing?"

Charlotte M. Mason, the brilliant and distinguished British educator at the turn of the century, wrote extensively about the development of self-government, or what she called the development of "the government of the kingdom of mansoul."[2] In her classic work on training and educating children, *Home Education*, she writes,

> In the outer of the three chambers sits the Will. Like that Roman centurion, he has soldiers under him: he says to this man, Go, and he goeth; to another, Come, and he cometh; to a third, Do this, and he doeth it. In other words, the *executive* power is vested in the will. If the will have the habit of authority, if it deliver its mandates in the tone that constrains obedience, the kingdom is, at any rate, at unity with itself. If the will be feeble, of uncertain counsels, poor Mansoul is torn with disorder and rebellion.[3]

The lack of a righteous and developed will, or *volition*, in the majority of men in America must be recognized as the underlying cause of the demise of our cultural stability. Men cannot lead themselves, much less anyone else. The rebellion they carry in their tripartite beings infects everything they attempt to oversee. Because of this the disease of anarchy is spreading rapidly in our day.

The Spread of Anarchy

The implications of the demise of self-government in men are staggering. Because men are appointed by God to provide servant leadership in the family, church, and state, these three institutions are slowly succumbing to the same anarchy their leaders have learned. Lawlessness appears to be rapidly emerging as the dominant sociological trend throughout Western culture. If anarchy rules in the heart of a man, he will infect everything he oversees with that same spirit.

Recently, within a brief ten-day period, I received several pieces of shocking news. First, I was informed that a Christian father whom I know had, only a couple of days earlier, walked out on his wife, leaving her and their four young children alone. He said he would not return. A few days later, the word came that a prominent Christian leader in a nearby city had resigned his post amidst an adulterous affair. Less than a week after this, a friend of ours told us that her sister's Christian husband had left her just the day before. She also has children at home.

All of these men are in their early thirties, and in each case there were two or more children left at home. One of the men was involved in an extra-marital affair, while in the other two cases, the men left simply because they wanted to. Each of these admitted to friends that what he was doing was wrong according to both the Bible and the laws written on his heart. At first two of the three were recalcitrant, unwilling even to speak to the pastors of their respective churches, though one is now involved in pastoral counseling.

The fundamental similarity is not their ages or demographics. The fundamental similarity is that each lacked self-government. Though each of these men claimed to be a Christian, he did not embrace an abiding commitment to bring his life under the lordship of Jesus Christ and His Father.

In our day it seems that most men, within the church and without, have at least a basic comprehension of morality and sin. No one has to tell them that raping and killing is evil or that cheating on your wife is considered immoral. Yet with each passing generation since the Industrial Revolution, the ability of the average man to walk in self-government has decreased incredibly to the point where now our actions no longer match our declared beliefs. We *think* right, and we *do* wrong.

The vast majority of Christian men whom I have known to be involved in pornography, for instance, have genuinely wanted to be set free from this sex addiction but have seemed incapable of simply walking away from it. Why? Because they have not been taught how to walk in self-government.

As the apostle James points out, it is not enough to know what is conceptually right; we must do the right thing or else we sin. More teaching, therefore, will not help the Christian man understand that lusting after one of the secretaries at work is wrong; he already knows that. He does not need more knowledge about morality; he needs to know how to "do the right thing."

Most men don't, and most men can't.

Turning on the Lights in the Barn

One of the questions that arise from this discussion is: "Can a child learn self-government on his own, or must he first experience some external government?" I think this is where fathering comes in. A wise father knows that his young son's spirit is not strong yet, and so he couples his stronger will with the weaker will of his son. By doing so he prevents the destruction that comes to the boy and others when self-government is lacking. This blessed phenomenon occurs only when there is enough authority in the father and enough of a love bond in the father-son relationship.

Overcoming the Weak Will

In days gone by, before fathering was despised and rejected as it is today, many men would develop self-government and a strong spirit under the testing of a father-son relationship. A typical training scenario might go like this:

In the early morning hours, before the sun is yet up, a young boy and his father sit at the breakfast table. Chores await them in the barn.

"Son," the father says, matter-of-factly, "I'd like you to head out to the barn and call in the cows for milking. Of course, you'll need to turn on the lights before you let 'em in. O.K.?"

The son, just eight-years-old, pauses. He looks up from his breakfast of toast and eggs and glances nervously out the window. Sheepishly he utters, "Dad, it's uh . . . kinda dark out there. Do you think you could go with me?"

Finishing his coffee, the father answers, "Sure, son. I'd be glad to. Let's go."

Together, the father and son clear their breakfast plates and stroll out across the yard toward the barn. A beaming full moon is occasionally overshadowed by massive black clouds as the light in the yard vacillates between dim and pitch black.

The young boy has walked this path with his father many times since last year. That's when Dad started having him do morning chores with him. But Dad had never asked him to go out to the barn and turn on the lights by himself. He wondered why his dad had changed the program today. At any rate, he is glad his father has agreed to go with him. "Who could ever do this alone?" he thinks.

Arriving at the barn, Dad again does something different. Typically, his father would tell the young lad to wait at the barn door while he walked the thirty or so feet to the light switch that was near the inside entrance to the milk house. It would be closer than walking all the way around the barn and directly entering the milk house from the east side.

But as they near the door, the father nonchalantly says, "Son, I'd like you to go on in and turn on the lights by yourself. I'll wait here by the door."

For the second time in less than ten minutes, the son feels a rush of fear come over him as he contemplates walking the long dark distance to the light switch. And again, he attempts to sound all grown up as he asks his father, "Dad, do you think you could go with me?"

"I think that would be O.K." the father replies, again with little hesitation. "Let's go."

With his dad leading the way through the nearly pitch blackness, the son struggles to follow close enough behind his father so as to monitor the sounds of his footsteps, but not so close as to bump into him. Unable to see a thing, the son begins to lose his bearings just about the time he hears his father start to hum a little. Comforted by the sound of his father's humming, he moves quickly in that direction. In a few seconds, the lights are on, and the two begin their chores.

The next day the scenario is repeated. Only this time the father walks with the son to the light but lets the young boy turn on the switch by himself. The next day the father stops a few feet short of the switch and asks his son to flip on the lights. After about a week, the son is walking most of the distance by himself as the father stands at the barn door. Each day the son's willingness to confront the darkness and go a little further by himself increases.

And then it happens.

In the early morning hours, before the sun is yet up, the young boy and his father are sitting at the breakfast table. Chores await them in the barn.

"Son," the father says, matter-of-factly, "I'd like you to head out to the barn and call in the cows for milking. Of course, you'll need to turn on the lights before you let 'em in. O.K.?"

The son looks up from his breakfast of toast and eggs and glances out the window at the darkness and says, "Sure, Dad. I'd be glad to."

Conclusion: Willing and Able

Ultimately, it is not enough that a man is *willing* to obey; he must also be *able* to obey. These two attributes, a willingness and an ability, are the vital foundations of the self-governed man. He *wants* to do what is right; he has set his will. And he is *able* to do what is right; his will is strong because he has been trained. His spirit is not only properly oriented in the direction of righteousness, but it is also hardy and well developed.

This man has been "working out" with his dad, his father pushing him a little each day, but never more than the son can bear. Each day the son's will grows stronger. Each day his confidence is increased. Each day he gains more ability to obey. Each day the mature strength of the father's spirit is being transfused into the son. And each day he moves closer to becoming a self-governed Kingdom Man.

Epilogue to Part II

Serving the King

We have now reached another turning point in our journey. Thus far, the focus has been on accepting the call to Kingdom Manhood on a personal level. Though the call to search for the King and to embrace natural fathers as helpers has been challenging, it is but the beginning. There is more, much more, to Kingdom Manhood than getting our personal lives in order. Kingdom order in a man's life is not an end; it is a means.

A revolution of Kingdom Manhood in America and all of the personal and cultural healing this would bring is possible, but seeing it become a reality will require some radical changes in the way Christian men think about their role. We are not called to introspective manhood. We are called to Kingdom Manhood. Implied in this call is the idea that we were created to serve a King, our Heavenly Father, and that it is His purposes in the earth, not ours, that we are destined to engage and promote. The nation we live in has turned its heart away from God, and it is our calling and destiny to see this nation's heart turned back.

As we embrace the good work of developing the life of the King within us, we must also embrace the good work of turning others to the righteousness of the Kingdom. Back on the path to Kingdom Manhood, we have some work to do.

Part III

Turning the Hearts

7.

Declaring a Kingdom Gospel

And this gospel of the kingdom shall be preached in the whole world for a witness to all the nations, and then the end shall come.

Matthew 24:14

In the modern sea of discordant themes and conflicting messages, Kingdom Men are appointed the task of declaring a pristine sound that resonates with the true male spirit. There are some notable counterfeits on the market, but only a King's Man can declare the authentic message of the ultimate sovereign One.

In preparing to turn the heart of America back to the Father, we must understand deeply what it is the Father wants us to proclaim to the people of this nation. What does He want us to tell them about Him? How does He want to be represented? If our message is erroneous, it will be thwarted. But if our message and the witness of our lives are truly declaring the Father's reign, we will see great fruit in the form of healed people, healed communities, and a healed nation.

Something's Been Missing

Large numbers of men in this country have taken a passing look at the church in America and have been turned off by what they see. This is not necessarily because they despise the things of Christ or the Bible. Rather, it is because they despise the watered-down, overfeminized, king-less gospel that the Western church offers them. In their search for ultimate truth, many men have tried American Christianity in some form at least once. Most have found it lacking something, but what it is they could not quite put their finger on.

Something has been missing in the message and the life of the Church, and this has caused many men to walk away. That missing something has been the gospel of the Kingdom, the message of a victorious King Who reigns for evermore and Whose Kingdom *was* inaugurated, *is* being advanced, and *will be* consummated at the end of the age. I believe that that missing something is about to be restored.

A Renewed Belief in the Father and His Kingdom

One hundred years from now, I think Christians will remember the twentieth century as the century of *restoration* for the Church. First, during the early 1900s, the ministry, power, and dynamics of the Holy Spirit was restored. The revival of the Holy Spirit was first noticed in the Pentecostal church, later giving birth to the charismatic movement.

After this, by about mid-century, the restoration moved forward to include the second part of the Trinity, the personhood of Christ. This phenomenon was clearly seen in the unusual emergence of what is now known as the Jesus movement. "Jesus People" were everywhere, and Jesus festivals dotted the countryside.

It is my firm conviction that a third restoration is coming in the days ahead, where we will see a renewed appreciation for the third person of the Godhead—the Father. As the concept of earthly fatherhood is progressively revived in society, and I believe it will be, worship of the heavenly Father will also see a revival. Predictably, this will bring with it a restoration in the belief of the Father's Kingdom. If the reinstallation of the Holy Spirit brought God's power, and that of Jesus brought God's salvation, then the recapturing of a theology of the Father, the head of the Godhead, will likely bring with it a renewal in the belief of God's reign.

Kingdom Manhood Requires a Kingdom Gospel

Every real man longs to meet a king, not a savior. Why? Because the Father set it up that way.

About two years ago, a young couple purchased the house across the street from us and became our new neighbors. When Mike and Denise first moved in, they were not Christians; in fact, they were not even married. Mike had grown up some in the church but rejected the religious scene as selfish hypocrisy. Though he inherently knew the Bible was true, he had no interest in getting "saved." He believed in God, but he had doubts about the church and the way it presented Christianity.

Mike's step-father, who is a friend of mine, encouraged Mike to attend a men's seminar I was doing in a nearby city. During the weekend Mike listened from a safe distance about seeking the King, developing self-government, and pursuing natural sonship. But it was not until I began to talk to the men about the gospel of the Kingdom that Mike finally started to take serious notice. The call for men to connect with the Father in His royal destiny of advancing His reign in the earth and the revelation that this is not only *permitted* by God, but is actually *expected*, was more than Mike could resist. He committed his life to Christ and to the Father that weekend and penned these words in a letter to me several weeks later:

> At the men's retreat, I finally learned what it really
> means to be a "Christian," and I like it. I have now
> made it my goal to be the best man of God I can be, the
> best husband and best father. I can't wait for the day
> when I am strong enough in God to kick the devil's tail
> the way he has kicked mine for the last twenty-four
> years. And I will reach my goal.

Like most men Mike was not looking to get "saved" in the
sense that the church had been presenting it. Rather, he was
looking to get *captured*—captured by a vision of a victorious
King Who has invited mankind, including Mike, to participate
in His glorious and royal destiny. Joining the "born-again" club
held little fascination for Mike, but joining a team of men and
women who were committed to seeking the Father's Kingdom
as a first priority became the life-giving vision for which Mike
had been unwittingly searching his entire life.

But What Is the Gospel of the Kingdom?

The original Kingdom Man was a Man consumed with the
gospel of the Kingdom; that is all He ever talked about. Consider the following: Jesus' first and last sermons declared the
Kingdom message (Matt. 4:17;28:18-20) as did His entire ministry. A great many of His parables began with the words, "The
Kingdom of heaven is like . . ." He said the Kingdom was being
taken away from Israel and given to a new nation—the Church
(Matt. 21:44; 1 Pet. 2:9). The Son of God warned that we
should not "shut up" His Father's Kingdom or prevent others
from entering it (Matt. 23:13). He said some of those living in
His day would not die until they had seen the inauguration of
the Kingdom (Mark 9:1). Christ sent the disciples out to tell
everyone about this Kingdom (Luke 9:2). He said the authority
of His Father's Kingdom did not originate *in* the earth (John
18:36), but expressed that He had all authority to govern *on*
the earth (Matt. 28:18). Jesus declared that the gospel of the
Kingdom must be preached *and* demonstrated throughout the
whole earth before the end would come (Matt. 24:14). And He
said that only those who were willing to do the will of His
Father could enter this Kingdom (Matt. 7:21).

Jesus, of course, was not the only New Testament radical

who spoke a lot about the Kingdom of God. John the Baptist preached the Kingdom before Jesus even began his public ministry, saying it was about to be revealed (Matt. 3:2). Paul preached the Kingdom throughout his missionary journeys (Acts 19:8); Philip preached the Kingdom (Acts 8:12); the apostle James preached the Kingdom (James 2:5); and Peter preached the Kingdom (2 Pet. 1:11). In fact, nearly every New Testament book makes some reference to the Kingdom of God and its centrality to the Christian life.

Nevertheless, the gospel or declaration of the Kingdom of God is something we hear precious little about in the Church these days. And when we do hear teaching on the subject, at least in most evangelical churches, the Kingdom is often presented as the *future* reign of Christ—the so-called Kingdom Age—and as having little present-day value. The Kingdom of God, though, is not limited to the Lord's *coming* dominion; it is a present-day governing reality to which the earth and all of us who live in it are currently being subjected. For the Kingdom of God is simply the *rule of God* . . . manifested now in a life, a family, a business, a church, a city, a nation.

In our Father's Kingdom, executive rule has been given unto Jesus Christ, who is now seated at the Father's right hand to reign under the Father's ultimate authority (Heb. 1:13). From His throne in His Father's presence, Christ will continue to rule until all of God's enemies have been abolished (1 Cor. 15:24-28).

If Christ is not the Father's present-day delegated King over the affairs of man on the earth, then He must have been either a liar or a fool when He said that He had *all authority on the earth* (Matt. 28:18). As far as I can tell, all authority *does* mean all authority, and this authority is not limited to rule over the Church; it is *all* authority. This means that He is presently reigning and will continue to do so until every lesser authority recognizes His sovereign reign and bends the knee.

Declaring the Kingdom gospel, then, is simply declaring the right and intention of God to rule in the everyday affairs of man *on the earth*. The Church will not embrace, and therefore will not promote, Kingdom Manhood until it has wrestled with and accepted this basic message. Because men are searching for a King, they will continue to bypass the Church that only presents a savior. They are no more interested in our self-help programs for men than the self-help programs the world offers. Until we declare the conquering King, men will continue to look elsewhere.

A King Has Conquered Your Land

Considering an idea from the world of antiquity may help us to understand the scope and impact of the Kingdom of God.

During the times of the ancient kings, when cities were walled high for protection, the idea of *covenant* had a more precise meaning than it does today. A covenant was the offer of an authority-vassal relationship that a conquering king would extend to a city within the borders of the region he had conquered. The king would send an ambassador and an army to proclaim his *gospel*—his sovereign declaration—to the cities of the conquered land and to extend his covenant *to* them and *over* them.

The solemn covenant (promise) would include the following five aspects:

1. the king's name, in whom the covenant was being authorized;
2. the history of the king as it relates to his current right to rule (the story of the conquest);
3. the expectations of the king (his royal law);
4. the sanctions of the covenant (consequences for obedience and disobedience); and
5. the duration of the covenant.[1]

The biblical parallels are not difficult to identify. The conquering King is Jesus, God's Son. The historical point of reference is the cross, for this is where our King defeated the ruler of the previous reigning power (Col. 1:13). The law of the King is the Ten Commandments, expounded upon by the rest of the Holy Scriptures. The sanctions, or blessings and curses, are overviewed in Deuteronomy 28 and detailed in other portions of the Bible. Finally, the duration of this new Kingdom is everlasting (Dan. 7:14).

If one thinks of the peoples of the earth as one large,

walled city still living under Satan's oppressive regime, though he has been conquered definitively and they could be set free, one can appreciate how the news of Christ's conquest over Satan (the gospel of the Kingdom) could be seen as very *good news*.

The Conquered Region Is the Earth

Jesus is a conquering King, and the region he has conquered is the earth. All authority on the earth, after all, has been rendered unto Jesus (Matt. 28:18-20), and He is presently reigning over the affairs of man (Eph. 1:21-23). Through His Church, He is working to bring all things under His lordship (Matt. 28: 19,20; Eph. 2:10) and to bring all things into rightful submission to His name (Phil. 2:10, 11). At some point in the future, Christ will return to earth, abolish death, and consummate His reign, at which time He will also turn the Kingdom back over to His Father (1 Cor. 15:24-28).

Jesus taught that Christians should pray daily for the Father's Kingdom to manifest itself *on the earth* (Matt. 6:10). His prayer was not "Thy Kingdom come, thy will be done in heaven" or "on Mars." He prayed, "Thy will be done on earth." Jesus understood that the issue is not getting the Father's will established in heaven; that is an accomplished fact. The issue is getting the Father's will established *on the earth*. Therefore, it is our job as Kingdom Men (and women) to declare the Kingdom of our Father to everyone who lives on the earth.

So Why Aren't We?

Many Christians assume that what the Church believes today is what the Church has always believed. This is especially true of believers who have been taught to think humanistically because we conclude that today's Church must be more advanced than the Church of centuries gone by. (Evolutionists, whether Christian or secular, always think this way.) If we do not hear much about the Kingdom as a present-day phenomenon, then it must not be relevant. Right? Wrong. The gospel of the Kingdom has been the mainstay of orthodox Christianity during most of the past two thousand years, even if this is not the case today. The gospel has not changed. We have.

Honey, I Shrank the Gospel!

Somewhere on the road to the twenty-first century, the gospel of the Kingdom diminished and was eventually replaced with the gospel of personal salvation. Welfarism, whether in the natural or in the spiritual, is not a biblical idea, but empowering people to reach their destiny in God is. Jesus said, "I am the way, and the truth, and the life; no one comes to the Father, but through Me" (John 14:6). In doing so Jesus declared that the objective of submitting our lives to Him was so that we could reach the Father. Jesus is the *way*, but pressing through to the Father is the *goal*. What the First Adam closed by his rebellion, the Second Adam (Jesus) opened by His obedience. This is why the veil in the temple was torn in two when Jesus died. His death reopened the way to the Father's presence.

For Kingdom Men the glorious appeal of finding Jesus Christ and His offer of forgiveness lies not in the self-centered focus of being saved from hell but in discovering the hitherto hidden pathway to the Father. For the Father's presence is where we find our destiny, our purpose, our life.

Today we see the Gospel presented as primarily a salvation issue: "come to Jesus, and He'll save you." Ironically, Jesus said that if we seek to *save* our life, we will *lose* it, but if we seek to lose our life for His sake, we will find it (Matt. 16:25). This paradoxical challenge necessitates that we approach Christ as dead men, ready to lay down our lives for Him and His Father, ready to pick up His cross (death) and follow Him into His Father's will, work, and Kingdom.

Nevertheless, this true gospel of the Kingdom has nearly vanished from the scene, and this is a tragedy. For until the Church recaptures the Kingdom message, we will not attract those who are truly seeking to enter the Kingdom. Catching what Jesus referred to as "violent men" (Matt. 11:12) requires that we preach the message Jesus preached and then open up the Kingdom for men seeking to "force" their way into it (Luke 16:16).

Weldon Hardenbrook has noted that in recent generations religion in America has come to be seen as a woman's concern.[2] At the same time this is happening, many men are progressively accepting the idea that there is a supreme *Authority*—a King. To their way of thinking, though, this King has little to do with the organized Church. Consequently, they must look elsewhere to find Him, which explains the phenomenal popularity of the secular men's movement, which unabashedly admits the existence of a "sacred king" and that "real men" must find him.[3]

It appears that Robert Bly is more willing to proclaim a Kingdom-like gospel than many in the Church. Though Bly leads men toward a false spiritual king, he is, nevertheless, connecting with something very fundamental in their hearts: their deepest desire to discover the highest authority available. Men will always pursue the King, whether through mythology and occult practices or via true Christianity. This reoccurring phenomenon is evident throughout the recorded history of man in both pagan and Christian cultures, and it is still true of men today. The problem, unfortunately, is that in the modern Western church, men are primarily being exposed only to the *salvation* of God, not His governing *authority*—His Kingdom. In their words, the Western church seems preoccupied with making converts, not submissive disciples.

When They Baptized Humanism

True biblical thinking came under serious attack in our country early in the 1800s by radical secular reformers who came out of the Enlightenment. The secular humanists, as they were to be called, openly declared war on the Church and the gospel of the Kingdom. This they did with the intention of separating society from the predominance and authority of the Church.

Christianity with its gospel of the Kingdom was, without doubt, the undergirding belief system in our country. The majority of citizens in this country believed that God reigned actively in the affairs of men and that this Kingdom rule was moving us toward a historical culmination of His purposes. God was in control. Though much of the historical studies done in our modern public schools seek to conceal this sociological truth, several Christian historians and scholars have been careful to preserve it. Francis Schaeffer, among others, notes the widespread nature of the Christian worldview at the time:

> The Christian world view, and biblical knowledge in particular, were widely disseminated throughout the culture and were a decisive influence in giving shape to the culture. In other words, at the time of the Reformation and in our country up until the last forty to sixty years, the large majority of people believed in basic Christian truths such as: the existence of God; that Jesus was God's Son; that there is an afterlife; that morality is concerned with what truly is right and wrong (as opposed to relative morality); that God is righteous and will punish those who do wrong; that there truly is evil in the world as a result of the fall; and that the Bible truly is God's Word.[4]

To the Humanist the Church was wrong in placing such unfettered emphasis on God and His sovereign rule. The emphasis, they held, should be on the more important issues of humanity, such as human accomplishments, human needs, human passions, and human potential. In their way of thinking, the Church's perspective of reality (the Christian worldview) was backward in that it placed God and his reign instead of mankind at the center of the belief system.

Humanism Goes to School

The Secular Humanists of the early 1800s had a passionate desire to move all of society, including the Church, in the direction of humanism. They had a strategy for how they could convert the masses, including the Christian masses, to their man-centered view of reality. They knew something that we in the Body of Christ seem to have forgotten: the one who controls the children controls the future. Men like Horace Mann, an avowed secularist, knew that if they were ever going to affect the way people think, they would have to gain access to their minds when they were very young.

Today's educational catastrophe is the fruit of their humanistic efforts. More important, today's amoral and immoral nightmare that we call modern American culture is also the fruit of their humanistic efforts. We are all the product of our educational system and philosophy. We are a humanistic society.

Though many in the Christian camp may have seldom considered the idea, any encyclopedia will tell us plainly that the intentions of those who promoted and constructed the public indoctrination system we now call the public schools did so with a secular vision of society in mind. The primary goal was never achieving excellence in education, though this rationale was thrown in for strategic value. Rather, the issue was always the separation of education from religion with the eventual goal of separating religion from society.

At a recent gathering of more than two hundred public school educators, entitled "Responding Democratically to Religious Agendas: Right-Wing Pressure Groups and School Reform," one plenary speaker openly admitted that this hidden agenda has long existed in the public school system. A Christian reporter who attended the conference noted that

> [He] acknowledged that humanist and secularist worldviews, or paradigms, are indeed present in the public school curricula. He mentioned that influential educator John Dewey was a self-described secularist who believed religious belief could be eradicated through proper education.[5]

The reporter quoted the speaker himself saying, "There is, in fact, a worldview that educators have inherited, through our study."[6]

During the mid 1800s, Charles Darwin's radical theories of evolution and the "survival of the fittest" added tremendous fuel to the already hot fires of humanism. Darwin's book, *The Origin of Species by Means of Natural Selection or the Preservation of Favored Races in the Struggle for Life*, published in 1859, posited that man was both self-created and self-developing. God, if He exists at all, has nothing to do with mankind; we are totally self-sufficient. This thinking eventually led to the related belief that morality, ethics, law, and values were also evolving or relative to the moment of time in question. The power and influence of humanism was beginning to gain momentum.

The Rise of Baptized Humanism in the Church

Humanism's anti-Kingdom-of-God philosophy eventually influenced the Church's thinking into the early 1900s. With most Christian children's being educated in the public school system, the Church began to drift ever so gently in the direction of a man-centered worldview. Within a few short generations, most of the new preachers and Christian college professors were being trained in the philosophies of humanism and would progressively attempt to synthesize Christian beliefs with humanistic theories.

Of this not-so-gradual shift, Schaeffer notes:

> In the late nineteenth century it was these ideas which began to radically transform Christianity in America. This started especially with the acceptance of the "higher critical" methods that had been developed in Germany. Using these methods, the new liberal theologians completely undercut the authority of Scripture. We can be thankful for those who argued strenuously against the new methods and in defense of the full inspiration and inerrancy of Scripture. One would remember especially the great Princeton theologians A. A. Hodge and B. B. Warfield, and later J. Gresham Machen. But in spite of the efforts of these men and scores of other Bible-believing Christian leaders, and in spite of the fact that the vast majority of lay Christians were truly Bible-believing, those holding the liberal ideas of the Enlightenment and the destructive methods of biblical criticism came into power and control in the denominations. By the 1930s liberalism had swept through most of the denominations and the battle was all but lost.[7]

This mingling of humanism with biblical Christianity eventually produced a more man-centered than God-centered view of God and the Bible. Humanism was being *baptized,* and the thinking of the Christian community was beginning to reflect it. Despite the Church's succumbing to the secularizing of society through the public school system, our defenses had already been weakened by an earlier form of religious humanism called pietism.

The pietists of the late eighteenth and early nineteenth

centuries held that the Christian should focus on spiritual things and the inner man. Contemplation of such secular foci as politics and the arts were regarded as pagan activities. This pseudo-spiritual emphasis caused much of the Church during this time to abandon the belief in the comprehensive reign of God in human affairs.

The Humanists pressed forward with their secular agenda, and many Christians were all too ready to retreat. One of America's top constitutional attorneys today, John Whitehead, describes some of the effects of pietism on the Church during this period:

> During the nineteenth century, humanists were thrusting their ideas into education, science, and the arts. Revivalistic piety, however, with its emphasis on the inner self, virtually abandoned these areas. Unfortunately, the church has been all too willing to use the categories of "secular" and "religious" when no such distinction exists in reality. All things have been created by God. Thus, all things have their origin in God and should be under Christ's lordship. The pietist renunciation thus raises a core issue: the *lordship of Christ*. To the true Christian, Christ cannot be Savior and not Lord. Christ is Lord over *all* areas of life—not merely the spiritual. Indeed, it is incorrect to make a fundamental distinction between spiritual and secular. Christ is Lord of the intellectual life, the business life, the political life. If Christ is not Lord over the arts and science, then man is. This is humanism in practice. If was difficult for the church to dispute humanistic ideology because the church itself was practicing humanism by separating the spiritual from the totality of life and reality.[8]

Birth of the One-Minute Christian

By the early part of this century, the Humanists had won the fight over whose worldview would undergird the culture. Christianity had been and still is relegated to the realm of "spiritual" ideas, and humanism has taken over to inform people how to think about the "secular" world.

Christianity devolved into an instantaneous, emotional experience instead of a life-long conscientious commitment.

Rather than challenging unbelievers to join us in laboring for the advancement of the Father's will in the earth, the Church caved in and became an inconsequential sales office selling condos in that eternal retirement village in the sky. Use of the altar call method of evangelism, first popularized by Charles Finney during the early-to-mid-1800s, was now widespread in evangelistic efforts, effectively turning Christianity into a one-minute emotional trip. Becoming a Christian took on a whole new meaning as the conversion experience became an end unto itself. Instead of the new birth's referring to the beginning of a new life under the reign of God, being "born-again" now meant you had uttered a "sinner's prayer" at the altar. "Presto change-o!, now you're a Christian. How do you feel?"

Adding insult to injury, many evangelists began to instruct that "every head be bowed and every eye be closed" during the altar call. Incredibly, the call to spiritual commitment became the call to spiritual cowardice as we unwittingly encouraged the non-Christian to *sneak* his way into the Kingdom while no one was looking. What a pitiful departure from the attitude of Jesus who called men and women to leave everything and publicly declare their allegiance to Him and His Father's Kingdom. Is it any wonder that most Christians in our day are afraid to share their faith in the real world? After all, they were born into Christendom in the fear of man.

The battle for the preservation of the true gospel was being lost. From the devilish womb of humanistic Christianity, the One-Minute Christian was born.

The Final Stages

By the turn of the century, the gospel of the Kingdom was in disrepute in most of Christendom while the gospel of humanism was growing in both the Church and the culture. At about the same time many mainline denominations were abandoning their belief in the inerrancy of Scripture, the Humanists were busy articulating their new gospel via their own sacred text: *The Humanist Manifesto* (the first of two, the second being the *Humanist Manifesto II*). While we were retreating from our biblically mandated care of widows, orphans, and foreigners, the secularists were filling the void with the creation of the welfare state. As fewer and fewer Christians became willing to dirty themselves with the hard work of managing our Father's earth, more and more non-Christians moved in to fill the political leadership vacancies. While we shipped our best and brightest off to seminary to prepare for the "ministry" of preaching, the Humanists sent their high achievers to Yale and Harvard to prepare for roles as movers and shakers in the culture. We were getting ready to leave, and they were getting ready to lead. We thought heaven. They thought earth.

The attitude of many Christians in America during much of this century has not been vastly different from that of many non-religious Humanists. Reading between the lines, we can see that the self-centered view of both groups is represented in the following words from the *Humanist Manifesto*:

> Though we consider the religious forms and ideas of our fathers no longer adequate, the quest for the good life is still the central task for mankind. Man is at last becoming aware that he alone is responsible for the realization of the world of his dreams, that he has within himself the power of its achievement. He must set intelligence and will to the task.[9]

A "baptized" version of the same lines might read as follows:

> Because we consider the religious beliefs of our fathers—that God's Kingdom should be our chief concern—no longer adequate, we now consider the quest for the good life to be our central task. We are at last becoming aware that Jesus has empowered us to realize our dreams, and by God's grace, we will do just that. We will set our will and intelligence to the task.

Humanism walked in and displaced Christianity as the prevalent worldview when we decided to give up our place near to the Father and His Kingdom's purposes. In doing so we gave up the culture, including the men of the culture, to the squatters who filled the void with the gospel of humanism. Nevertheless, by God's grace, this is going to change.

Conclusion: Embracing the Right Message

Only as the Church returns to its job of declaring the Father's Kingdom reign will the men of America find in the Church the message their hearts are programmed to hear. It is the only message that prepares men to meet God. The sound of self-centered, humanistic Christianity—come to Jesus and He will *save* you—will continue to fall silent on the ears of men who are listening for the call to true righteousness and personal destiny.

John the Baptist raised the King's banner as he ministered by the Jordan River before Jesus came to earth the first time. The Bible tells us of his preparatory calling:

> And he will turn back many of the sons of Israel to the LORD their God. And it is he who will go as a forerunner before Him in the spirit and power of Elijah, to turn the hearts of the fathers back to the children, *and the disobedient to the attitude of the righteous; so as to make ready a people prepared for the LORD* (Luke 1:16,17, emphasis added).

John's message was clear and succinct: *"Repent, for the Kingdom of heaven is at hand"* (Matt. 3:2). If we as Kingdom men are serious about turning disobedient men into the righteous, we will need to embrace and declare the same message—the gospel of the Kingdom.

8.

Embracing the Call to Fatherhood— The Leadership Mandate

O My People! Their oppressors are children, and women rule over them. O My People! Those who guide you lead you astray, and confuse the direction of your paths. The LORD arises to contend, and stands to judge the people. The LORD enters into judgment with the elders and princes of His people.

Isaiah 3:12-14a

Kingdom men are called to *leadership*.

The very word *leadership* invokes images—Winston Churchill, King David, Ulysses S. Grant, Attila the Hun, Lee Iacocca, Joshua, Abraham Lincoln, Martin Luther, Martin Luther King, Jr., Moses, Norman Schwartzkopf . . . Jesus Christ. On a less grandiose scale, when many people think of leadership, their pastor comes to mind, or a senior business executive they happen to know, or the current president. It is no wonder I get the following reaction from male audiences wherever I speak.

Any Celibates in the House?

"I want to ask you a simple question," I often start off. "How many of you consider yourself a Christian leader?" Routinely, about a third to one-half of the men will usually raise their hands, some more slowly than others.

"Now, of those who did *not* raise your hands—you do not consider yourself a Christian leader—how many of you believe you are called to celibacy?" Beginning to realize they have been set up, and having no intention of pursuing life alone, no one ever raises his hand.

So what is the point? Most of us men do not consider ourselves to be Christian leaders, even though virtually all of us are either married or planning to be married. Sadly, this implies at least indirectly that we do not esteem the familial role of fathering on the same level as Christian leadership. Or, more to the point, we usually do not think of Christian leadership when we think of fatherhood. Though the Bible speaks much about the leadership responsibilities of a father, we invariably equate Christian leadership with something other than fatherhood. This is in spite of the fact that God Himself, the overarching leadership figure of humankind, speaks of Himself as *the Father*.

Obviously, Christian leadership encompasses more than the family, but does it encompass more than fatherhood?

Fatherhood: The Essence of True Leadership

When one thinks of fatherhood, one often considers the relationship a dad would have with his kids, and well one should, for fatherhood begins in the family. But fatherhood cannot be limited to the family. In a larger sense, fatherhood is a biblical and historically honored leadership paradigm. From antiquity it has been the model and standard for all true leadership, not familial leadership only.

For instance, the head of the triune God, the One who is leading all mankind toward its corporate destiny, is referred to as the Father. The Apostle Paul spoke of himself as a father in relation to whole churches who were not his biological progeny; of his helpers, Timothy and Titus, as beloved sons though they were not his biological children. Appropriately, we remember the founders of our communities as city fathers. The Old Testament is replete with hundreds of references to Israel's past national and tribal leaders as fathers. The Roman Catholic church reveres its pastors and priests as fathers. We teach our children that America was conceived and built through the vision, selfless sacrifice, and commitment of our founding fathers. We have the early church fathers. Senators in ancient Rome were called fathers. Even Jesus carried the honored name of Everlasting Father (Is. 9:6).

But What Is Fatherhood?

A father is a leader, but he is more than just a leader. Anyone can lead. Webster says a *leader* is simply a "... person ... that leads."[1] A leader is anyone who can master the skills that attract followers. Where he leads his people— toward heaven or away from it—may become a secondary issue.

Hitler, for instance, was a tremendous leader with an unquestionably substantial ability to motivate millions of people to follow him, and yet we see that he led his followers into some of the greatest corporate atrocities the modern world has ever seen. Hitler was a great leader to Nazi Germany, but he was never a father.

Leading others then can be for good or for evil. This is why a certain type of leadership must be called out as the standard. That which is needed is fatherhood. As a leadership paradigm, fatherhood embodies the godly idea of assuming full responsibility for the welfare of one's followers. Whereas humanistic leadership focuses on the estate of the leader, fatherhood focuses on the estate of the followers. The two are diametrically opposed.

Christ gave us the perfect example of the father-like leadership God expects from Christian men. He willingly laid down His very life so that His followers could find life. His concern was for the welfare of those He was called to lead. His high priestly prayer demonstrated the selfless love of a father's heart as He asked God the Father to take care of His disciples after His departure—to "keep them" (John 17). This was the perfect love of the Father above being expressed through His faithful Son.

Biblical fatherhood also embodies the idea of blessing those for whom you are responsible. Their welfare must come first. In their book, *The Blessing*, Gary Smalley and John Trent identify five basic elements of this blessing, which they call the "family blessing."[2] They are:

- meaningful touch (that accompanies the blessing);
- a spoken message (an audible blessing);
- attaching "high value" to the one being blessed;
- picturing a special future for the one being blessed (a visionary blessing); and
- an active commitment to fulfill the blessing.

Only one who is aimed at serving his followers can provide this blessing.

Fatherhood is the highest calling of leadership. It embodies faithfully stewarding other people for the Father Himself and leading them toward His presence. These may be children or employees, a project team at work or at church, a congregation or an entire congressional district, the citizens of a city or even an entire nation—on any and every level, the father-leader is essential.

Only Fathers Can Turn Their Hearts

Historically, when law and order begin to break down in a society, the demand for a strong king intensifies. When people cannot rule themselves, they will demand that someone else rule them. This phenomenon can be clearly seen in the inner cities of our nation. As the plight of fatherless boys increases, so does the interest and involvement in street gangs. These men, too young to govern themselves yet and having no fathers to provide godly leadership to them, will naturally be attracted to strong gang leaders as fathers, as earthly kings.

This is true on a larger scale in America as well. The 1992 presidential elections bore this out as Ross Perot took a high percentage of the popular vote (unusual for a third-party candidate) due to the widely held perception that both George Bush and Bill Clinton were inadequate leaders. A nation without a fatherly president—a man who could instill in the heart of the citizenry the sense that he was watching out for their needs—almost elected a national "gang leader" to rule over us. As we head toward future elections, we are increasingly vulnerable to a demagogic takeover because our country continues to decline in nearly every recognized measurement.

If we do not give them fathers, men who lead them toward heaven, they will continue to settle for "great" leaders, like Hitler. And great leaders who are not fathers will more often than not lead their followers to hell. Surely, this is where our nation is heading.

The author Weldon Hardenbrook believes that the lack of fatherhood is at the very heart of the cultural crisis:

> I humbly but firmly submit that the soul of our nation is in crisis in large part because American men have—from ignorance and for various and sometimes even subconscious reasons—abandoned their God-given role of fatherhood. They have discarded the notion of being responsible for the physical and spiritual well-being of those around them.[3]

Fatherhood must again become the standard of leadership. In the truest sense, the real federal deficit in this country is not the one measured in dollars and cents; it is the one measured in father-like leaders. The deficit is staggering.

The passionate exhortation of the prophet Malachi centers first on the strategy of "turning the hearts of the fathers to the children . . ." and *then* "turning the hearts of the children to their fathers" (Mal. 4:6). In this way God is calling the leaders, all of them, to turn their attention to their followers and away from themselves. This is a biblical curse-abating strategy. What if the Christian businessman, for example, were to expand his business, not relative to the market demand, but relative to the number of employees for whom he could genuinely pray each day? Like a good father, the business owner would bring each employee by name before the throne of God in intercession, even as Christ did for His team. This would require him to take the time to get to know each employee personally. The businessman would likely reach his maximum quickly, probably around ten or so employees; at which point, if he wanted to continue to grow, he would have to raise up a "son" who would also begin praying for a portion of the team, and so forth.

What if this same Christian businessman chose his employees the way Christ did His disciples, by praying all night before deciding (Luke 6:12,13)? Both of these strategies would likely cause the business to grow more slowly, but so what? Christ's new "business" grew very slowly at first, too. For the initial three years of laying the foundation, His primary work team grew to include only twelve men (and He was God!). But once the foundation was well laid, the church exploded, and it has been "in business" ever since.

Fathering, as a leadership strategy, needs to be employed across the cultural landscape. Only as the dads of our land turn away from cowardly, lazy, and pleasure-seeking ways and turn their hearts instead to the desperate and fatherless cries of their children will the family begin to be rebuilt. Only as the pastors of our communities forsake the self-glorifying ambitions set before them by a devilish society and start considering the whole community as their congregation, reaching out to the people as if they were children lost without parents, caring for them with the heart of a father, will the Church begin to see restoration and religious renewal.

Only as business owners and department managers of our corporate institutions forsake worshipping the almighty dollar and begin to serve their employees as if they were sons and daughters in a family-owned business will we begin to restore our commercial viability in the global market place. Only as judges who sit on the benches of our land become willing to view each criminal who comes before them as a little child caught in the act and commit themselves to disciplining them with a righteous mix of grace, justice, and Solomonic wisdom will we see peace return to the judicial system. Only as lawmakers and the political executives of our civil arena turn from lust for power and money and begin to view each constituent as if he were part of a large family will we begin to see a government of the people, by the people, and most important, *for* the people. Only as the nation forsakes self-serving leadership models and returns to fatherhood will the curse on our land truly be removed. As men again begin to recapture fatherhood on the family level, they will naturally export this godly style of leadership to the other realms they oversee. One cannot be a true father at home and a self-serving tyrant at work. One cannot care for one's own children without feeling paternal concern for the members of the church family one pastors. After learning to love and lead like fathers in the home, men will discover that they have taken that same leadership paradigm into their political arenas. Fatherhood, once experienced on the family level, will start to emerge as the dominant directional force on every level.

When this occurs our nation will begin to see healing.

Fatherhood—The Ultimate Standard for Leadership

In the post-modern world of Western culture, the belief in fatherhood as the true leadership standard and model has obviously been misplaced, lost in a day of humanistic nonsense. Since the advent of the Industrial Revolution, a leader is no longer one who cares for, provides for, and protects his followers. Having passed the bicentennial mark of this post-enlightenment experiment we call American culture, a leader is no longer one who thinks of his employees or his constituents or even his parishioners as his children. In fact, as we near the end of the millennium, and perhaps the end of our national stability as well, many a man who actually begets children no longer thinks of himself as a father. He is perhaps a boyfriend, or the one who pays for the abortion, or a roommate, or a domestic partner, but not a father. Fatherhood has been attacked, has fallen, and has been replaced.

But all of this talk of fatherhood and leadership paradigms may seem rather irrelevant to some men, for they are still not sure if it applies to them. Unless a man believes he is called to leadership, the issue of *how* he leads, fatherly or otherwise, is a moot point. So we must now ask the male reader a question, "Are you called to leadership?"

The Call to Father—Lead a Family

Until a man settles the issue that he is called to leadership on some level, he will be unsure of his destiny and less motivated to fulfill his call in life because every man's destiny is inseparably tied to that which he is called to lead. Adam was incomplete without Eve; David would have been quite limited without his thirty mighty men; Jesus could not have fulfilled His call to build the foundation of the Church without the twelve Disciples; Paul would have been hampered in his missionary efforts without Timothy and Titus. A man cannot reach his potential in Christ without finding those who are called to work with him.

Second, until a man embraces a *vision* of himself as a leader, he will not be motivated to do the hard work of becoming a King's Man; he will settle for simply becoming an adult male. Why? Because without a vision the people perish or become unrestrained (Prov. 29:18), and the vision that motivates a man to press on in life is leadership; he is simply wired that way because this is the role God created him to play.

For nearly all men, then, leadership begins with leading a family. Though many men have some difficulty seeing themselves as aspiring to community leadership, nearly every man believes he is called to marriage. Based on this statistical reality, we must conclude that nearly every man is called to lead something—a family.

Rebuilding the Culture Takes Families

The call to rebuild our nation is first a call to rebuild our families. Without a strong family base in our culture, we will not have the strength to rebuild our cities because the workers required need to emerge from strong families. Let me illustrate.

In Nehemiah's day, the walls that surrounded Jerusalem were broken down, and the gates were burned with fire. Nehemiah was moved by God to rebuild the walls of that once great city. Though the story of the reconstruction of the walls is a true historical account, it also has significant symbolic meaning for us in the spiritual rebuilding of our cities and nation. The walls speak of protection for the people. Their fallen estate and the imagery of the breaches where the enemy could come through tells of a lack of safety and a sense of vulnerability. In our day personal safety, whether for one's body, soul, or spirit, is at a premium, and in some families or cities, it is not available at any cost. Truly the walls lie in ruin in our nation.

The gates were the places where the elders would sit in counsel and provide government or orderly oversight for the city. The picture of the gates being burned with fire speaks of the collapse of godly leadership for the people. Certainly this is true of our day on at least two levels: the "elders" have abandoned the family gates and the city gates. Because of this all manner of evil is permitted to pour into our families and cities. It is no longer necessary for the enemy to climb over the fence to kill, destroy, and steal (John 10:7-11); he can go right through the unattended gates and get at our families or the citizens of our cities. There are few elders present to protect the people; the gates are empty.

So how did Nehemiah organize his rebuilders? This is a key question because if we fail to recognize his organizational strategy we will miss the genius of this master builder's plan.

Instead of forming a steering committee, a masonry task force, a gate-builders' union, a factory for making mortar, and a rubble-removing corporation, Nehemiah simply put the laborers to work on the wall in front of their own homes. The rebuilding process was inherently *family-based*. Each family or clan was responsible for rebuilding a section of the wall relative to their resources and ability. Many families built only short sections, while one family group had adequate means to rebuild more than fifteen hundred feet of the wall and hang the large Valley Gate. So the labor of the reconstruction effort relied totally upon the strength of the individual family.

This approach makes a lot of sense because building the wall in front of one's own house has a way of motivating one to work hard and do a quality job. A man's future protection would rely upon the structural integrity of the wall he had built in front of his own home.

I have often wondered what Nehemiah would have done if the family in his day had been as dysfunctional as it is in ours. What social unit would he have called upon to do the building if the families were in shambles? When the workers became discouraged, how could he have appealed to them on the basis of rescuing their wives and children from the surrounding enemies (Neh. 4:14) if they had already been lost through divorce or did not have any children to protect because they had bought the childless-is-best nonsense we were all taught so well by Margaret Sanger and her pathological Planned Parenthood peddlers?

A large part of the emotional fuel that Nehemiah used related to the father's sense of protection for his relatives. Nehemiah challenged them flat-out to fight for their family's survival. He seemed to know what we seemed to have forgotten—without the family unit, there will be no rebuilding, no walls, no safe city, no city gates, no orderly government in the city. The city will remain in ruins, and chaos will reign. The people will live in great distress and reproach.

Rebuilding the Family Takes Fathers

America's families are desperate for fathers.

Even political leaders are beginning to see the need for a revival of fatherhood at the family level. The former Deputy Director of Public Liaison in the Reagan administration, Don Eberly, thinks the White House and Congress should restructure their approach to the cultural crisis. When asked by a reporter about the bandied-about term, "family values," and the role they play in American politics, Mr. Eberly said, "The real issue is missing men, and the crisis in this culture is a crisis in fatherhood. You can't reach a father through legislation."[4]

Asked next, "How can we reach fathers?" Eberly replied,

> We have to develop a men's movement in this country. A social movement that has little to do with politics and legislation. A movement designed to awaken renewed concern among men about their responsibility for children. To restore pride, the rewards, the dignity and the sense of respect that comes with caring for one's own children.[5]

Do we need a "men's movement" in this country? Perhaps so, but if we do, the men's movement that we need is a movement of men toward fatherhood starting with fathering their families.

In America's agricultural past, the national work force was largely organized around family-based enterprises—a *father-based* enterprise. A man's work environment was typically either the family farm or a family-based service sector job that supported the farming industry, such as carpentry or operating the country store. The close proximity of fathers to their families was healthy for everyone involved, and the strength of our culture was intrinsically tied to the strength of our families. Fathers stood between the family and the forces that would have destroyed it. In the spiritual realm, we built incredibly high walls around our nation, walls that protected us from the enemy of our nation's soul, and we did it one family at a time. By every measure we were stronger then.

Yet as we entered the Industrial Revolution, the work force began to shift away from the family-based enterprise system and toward the factory-based economy. Most people who worked spent their days either in the factory setting or in some service sector job that supported the emerging industrial communities, not the farm. When men left the farm, they more or less left their families. When men left their families, they more or less left fatherhood.

Back to the Farm?

Must we then return to the farm? Must we go back into America's past and capture the simpler life of living off the land in some rural hideaway? Must we chuck city life, even suburbia, and head for the prairies of the Midwest or the corn fields of the Northeast? Must we somehow go back in time and recapture the "good ole days" of the 1840s?

The issue is not returning to the farm; the issue is returning to the *family*. Men must turn their attention back to leading their wives and children. Career must come second. Ministry must come second. Hobbies must come second. Watching football must come second. Golfing must come second. Everything, other than a man's relationship with his Father, his personal time with God, must be placed as a lower priority than father-leading his family. This may sound radical, but then again, biblical Christianity has always been a radical concept.

A man is commanded to love his wife as he loves his own

body (Eph. 4:28). How can he do this if she falls to a lower priority than his own desires? A man is called to train up his children in the Lord (Eph. 6:4) and to teach them both morning and night in the things of God (Deut. 6:7), but how can he do this if he puts his career or his hobbies or watching television ahead of spending time with his kids? How many Christian men do you know that invest an hour or more a day in the Word and in prayer, let alone train their children or lead their wives in God's way out of their resulting revelation? I am sure there are a few, but if there are many, it is one of the best kept secrets in the body of Christ.

Like Christ we must put our families first. Jesus interceded for His disciples before the Father's throne and therefore was called a high priest. Jesus also took tremendous amounts of time away from His public ministry to personally teach His disciples in the ways of God. Jesus apprenticed His disciples so that they would be experienced in the work for when He left. In the end Jesus made the ultimate sacrifice in that He gave up His very life for His disciples. This is the way of a father. This is the way of fatherhood.

We men must accept as our first Christian responsibility the call to build strong Kingdom families: families where the government and peace of God are evident (Is. 9:7); families where the joy of God reigns in our children and in our wives; families where each member is consciously pursuing biblical self-government under the lordship of Jesus Christ; families where the ministry of the Holy Spirit is welcomed in healing, in leading us into all truth, and in comforting us; families where the beliefs of the Bible, the principles of the Kingdom, are being taught daily and tenaciously; families where the royal life of the Kingdom of God is demonstrated for a witness unto the nations (Matt. 24:14).

If we will accept this call, the family, at least in the Christian community, will begin to be rebuilt. These families will progressively emerge as the foundation for the rebuilding of the walls in the culture.

Rebuilding the Family Takes Radical Thinking

There are some changes ahead for men who accept the call

to fatherhood on the family level. All of them are for the better, but most will not be realized without some pain.

One of the many areas this challenge will ultimately touch is how we men structure our occupational pursuits. I would like to humbly suggest that the opportunity to organize our careers around the family-based enterprise concept is greater today than it has been in nearly a century. With the advent of the personal computer, the FAX machine, laser printing, modems, cellular phones, and a host of other technological wonders, many occupations now being pursued through the large or medium-sized-corporation could be converted to family-based ones. I have seen attorneys, construction workers, pastors, computer programmers and technicians, auto mechanics, dentists and physicians, educators, researchers, writers, artists and musicians, administrators, and clerical workers transform their career status from employee to entrepreneur.

This is not to say that the work environment will necessarily be home-based, although in many cases it may be. Rather the enterprise becomes *family-based*, meaning the organizational foundation for the business is the family, not the impersonal corporation. The family *owns* the business.

When a business becomes family-owned, the opportunity for shared vision and shared responsibility among the family members is increased. If the impersonal corporation that Daddy works for goes into bankruptcy, for instance, the family has a certain amount of motivation to pray because of Dad's job security. But if the family business starts heading for financial failure, the prayers and the involvement reach a whole new level of intensity because losing the family business is like losing a part of the family's vision and identity. It is different than just a job. The family-based enterprise becomes a part of the family, like an extra member.

Many Christian men dream about finding and marrying a woman like the Proverbs 31 woman, the virtuous woman. But do we realize that the enterprise this incredible woman oversaw was a family-based business, and the woman's husband, qualified by his successful family-based enterprise and well-ordered family, was off sitting in the city gates as a city elder? Why would God bless us with a modern-day business wonder woman when we do not need one?

The family-based enterprise is a radical thought, of course, and in many situations it may simply not be feasible. Nevertheless, I hope that many men reading this will be challenged to reexamine their rationale for basing their occupational ambitions outside the family and will, in general, open themselves up to a willingness to think radically about what it will take to restore fatherhood to their families. After all, the word "radical" may not be as radical as it sounds. It simply means to get to the root of things, and this is exactly what we men need to do: get to the root of what it will take to father-lead our families.

Answering the Call Takes "Real Men"

The call to leadership is sure for most men, and it begins in the family. God designed it that way so that men would learn to lead others like a father. The question now becomes "Will men answer the call?"

Answering the call to father-lead a family will mean that we carefully and wisely steward each member of the family team as a relational *trust* given to us by Christ to help us in advancing His Kingdom and for which He will expect an accounting when He returns. Like Jesus with His disciples, our job as fathers and husbands is to lead each member of the team toward his destiny in the Father (John 17:21), toward discovering his own Kingdom vocation in this life. We cannot drop or lose any of the team players that the Father has called us to "keep." Answering the call will ultimately mean that we embrace a bottom-line biblical truth: Unless he is called to celibacy, leading a family is the first leadership task of every Kingdom Man. Period.

The Call to Father-Lead a Community

As we have seen, the call to father-lead a family is essential to the rebuilding of the nation. The family is the first place where a man learns to lead people, to give an account of the relational trust, and to try his hand at real fatherhood. But it is not the only place. Proven fathers are called to lead beyond the borders of the family. They are called to father-lead a community. This means that after they have proven themselves as faithful fathers in the realm of the family, they can now be called to lead larger groups of people. This may be a handful of employees in a family-based enterprise, a large hospital staff, or maybe even an entire city.

Who's Watching the Hen House?

I have noticed something. In my home city, the political arena is dominated by people who reject Christianity and biblical ethics. Included in this category of non-Christian rulers are the entire city council and the mayor, the city police chief and most of the majors in the department, an estimated twenty-five out of twenty-nine county legislators and the county executive, the county district attorney, the entire sitting judiciary on the city, county, and state supreme courts, all of our state senators and assembly representatives, our state attorney general, our congresswomen, both of our U.S. senators, and, of course, our president and his entire cabinet. Within these ranks there are certainly some who would consider themselves conservative on many cultural issues (although there is not a conservative majority in any of the realms I just mentioned with the exception of our local county legislature). Nevertheless, the number of professing Christian evangelicals who serve as senior political leaders in or representing my home city is nearly zero. And this is just the civil arena.

As I have talked with Christian leaders in the business sphere of our community, I have discovered that things are not much better there; the top leadership posts are generally held by those who oppose Christian values. Even the service sector and the non-profit corporations are dominated by non-believers. Most of the family service agencies are non-Christian led, as is the main community chest organization (United Way), the primary food bank groups, the agencies reaching orphaned and troubled children, the mental health care services, the hospitals, the adult group homes, the elderly care facilities, and so forth. The major media in my city, of course, are also controlled by non-believers, as are the local televisions stations and most of the radio stations.

Where are all the Christian leaders in the community? Are we Christians less intelligent? Are the unbelievers natural born leaders and we natural born followers? Did God ordain that community leadership on any serious level must be conducted by those who reject Him and His law?

One of Australia's great Christian leaders, Tom Marshall, holds that leadership, by definition, is better suited for the Christian than the unsaved. In his sterling book, *Understanding Leadership*, he argues that the Christian community should be able to produce "more and better leaders than any other section of human society."[6] This, he says, is because true leadership is the ability to have vision and guide people toward that vision:

> We are future oriented, we are the people that belong to the future and to whom the future belongs because we belong to the Lord who holds the future.[7]

Our problem is not poor qualifications; our problem is poor theology. Because we have been taught a get-'em-saved-and-get-'em-out-of-here gospel, we have come to believe that senior leadership in the community is a waste of time. Who would ever get saved because I became a county court judge? Who would ever get saved because I became the local chief of police? Who would ever get saved because I served my way into the CEO position at Kodak over a twenty-year period? Who would ever get saved because I became a member of the school board? Who would ever get saved because I became the owner of one of the local television stations? Who could ever get saved because I decided to spend the next four years in Congress trying to help America balance its corporate checkbook? Who would ever get saved because I took my spot among the leaders of the community? Frankly, I think millions of people would.

Why is street evangelism falling on its face these days? It is largely because the average Joe walking down the street no longer has any foundation for hearing our message because his *leaders* have led him astray. He was likely raised on value-free education, destiny-less evolutionary theory, anti-Christian bigotry, socialistic fascism, and MTV. For decades his brain has been pummeled with images of insatiable sex, violent barbarity, and unfettered hedonism. He is the modern man. He may not be able to read, but at least he knows how to use a condom.

Can you see the problem? Because we have come to worship quick-fix evangelism and out-of-touch Christianity, we have given the culture away. Can any sane person argue rationally against the reality that true evangelism flows more freely and obtains greater results in a country where the righteous rule? Look at Eastern Europe since the fall of communism. The masses are turning to Christ in Moscow, not because they have better evangelistic techniques, but rather because the oppressive regime that sought to silence the Church is gone (at least temporarily). Who should be watching the hen house? The Bible says *we* should.

> When the righteous triumph, there is great glory, but when the wicked rise, men hide themselves. (Prov. 28:12)

> When the righteous increase, the people rejoice, but when a wicked man rules, people groan. (Prov. 29:2)

Where's an Elder When You Need One?

As it stands now, our city "gates" are abandoned and burned with "fire." All manner of unspeakable evil is being allowed to pour into our communities unchecked. Justice has fallen in the streets, and Darwin's survival-of-the-fittest ideology is emerging as the barbaric rule of the day. This is not because of the rise of anti-Christ or some other apocalyptic inevitability. Rather, it is because our cities lack godly elders.

Even though your city and mine has elected officials, most cities have no true elders. The elders are those righteous leading men who are called by God to gather as servants to bring justice to the city. These are the senior men who have proven themselves faithful to the Father and their followers, first on the family level and then in the sphere of their community leadership. This may include pastors, business leaders, politicians, and attorneys. As these men establish themselves in their respective spheres, they should progressively turn their attention to the city gates. In time, they should engage service that brings godliness and righteousness to the community at large. This will require that they begin to use their abilities and resources for the good of the community, not just their own good. This, of course, is what a father would do anyway.

One of the leading Christian strategists in our nation, Dennis Peacocke, has written extensively on the concept of calling Christian men as elders to the "city gates." In his book, *Winning the Battle for the Minds of Men,* he writes:

> Leaders in Old Testament Israel understood their political responsibility "to sit in the gates of the city," overseeing the quality of life within. This honor was the ultimate civil place of esteem. If the thief or the unscrupulous business-man destroyed or cheated the inhabitants of the city, the inhabitants had the right to challenge the elders as to why such men were let into the city in the first place. The elders were God's first line of defense for the safety and welfare of the people. The elders judged as the duly constituted legal rulers. God held those elders responsible both for the continued well-being of the citizens and also for protecting the citizens from evil without the gates.[8]

The call to fatherhood begins in the family and extends to the city gates. We desperately need fatherly leaders looking out for the welfare of the citizens of our communities.

But Where Will We Find Them?

Because most Christian men do not aspire to senior lead-ership spots in the community, we presently lack Christian leaders on the intermediary level. Consequently, the pool of available elders is incredible shallow. Nevertheless, to restore justice to our communities and to protect our cities from the wicked and perverse who are trying to destroy the citizens, we need men who have proven themselves capable of father-lead-ing something on this level—a business, a department in the corporation, or a church.

Many Christians bemoan the situation in our civil govern-ment. We are vexed by ever increasing taxes, abortion-on-demand, laws against Bible-reading and prayer in school, and so forth. But why is the civil sphere dominated by those the Bible refers to as pagans,[9] those who reject our Lord's teach-ings? Why are we basing our laws on relativism instead of time-honored biblical truth?

Peacocke says the elders have abandoned the gates:

> The secular state, through the Church's default, holds the upper hand right now. It has grown in direct proportion

to the Church's withdrawal. It has sought, largely uncontested, to establish itself in the eyes of the people as the true shepherds and caretakers of their welfare. It has co-opted the Church and in many ways demanded to do the Church's true work. Why shouldn't it, since much of the Church withdrew from pastoring the nations?[10]

The same holds true for the commercial realm, education, the arts, media, and nearly every other dimension of the culture. Christians seldom aspire to senior leadership spots, and the resulting vacuum has been filled by the ungodly.

Conclusion: America Is Desperate for Fatherhood

The great question today is whether there exists in the Christian church a sufficient reservoir of spiritual strength with the capacity to throw up leaders of the right calibre to meet the challenge of the present leadership vacuum.[11]

The call to fatherhood encompasses the call to lead in the family *and* in the community. It is the challenge to take the fatherly leadership skills acquired and tested in the home out into the workplace, wherever that might be. It is the call to maximize one's leadership ability and opportunities for the Father, to bring His care into every community situation where oversight is required and to seek to extend His Kingdom by extending the influence of His sons. We are in desperate need of men willing to accept this call.

The fact that the populace continues to embrace the erroneous notion that civil government can and should solve every national problem we face only demonstrates the degree to which the people have become blinded by the deadly lies of socialistic humanism. In reality the involvement of Caesar in matters that God never intended for Caesar to touch will always produce demonic fruit. After all, Caesar is only blessed by God when he stays within his appointed realm. When he moves beyond his calling, he moves beyond the realm of God's anointing, and we all suffer the consequences.

Ultimately, though it may sound utterly simplistic and uncomplicated to the sophisticated Western mind, the greatest need our nation has is for more fatherly men willing to lay down their lives for those whom they lead. This is the key to turning hearts. For it is not *whether* one leads; it is *how* one leads. If fatherhood is good enough for God, then it is good enough for me.

9.

Fostering the Revolution

*Let your light shine before men in such a way that they may
see your good works, and glorify your Father who is in heaven.*

Matthew 5:16

It is time for *next steps* thinking. Where does the aspiring
Kingdom Man go from here?

Changing the Course of a Nation

A consultant friend of mine once told me, "Doing today
what you've always done is the perfect strategy for achieving
the results you've always gotten." But like most of my associ-
ates, I often think that *time* alone will correct the problems we

face as a nation. Tomorrow will be different; things will be better. It is the reasoning of American optimism, an unquenchable faith in the American dream. But will things improve if we simply "stay the course"?

The "course" we have set as a nation is proving to be a disastrous one. As long as we continue to hold to the underlying principles of humanism, whether we do this under the guise of Christianity or secularism, our culture will progressively lose its corporate life. Ideas have consequences, and the idea of self-worship leads to the consequence of death (Matt. 16:25). If you seek to save your life, whether "you" are a nation, a family, a business, a city, a church, or an individual, you will lose it.

Though scores of Christians are beginning to see the signs of our nation's progressive decline, many do not know, in a fundamental way, what we must do differently to change things. We do not know the recipe for revolution. Consequently, many of us coast along with the masses hoping that something or someone will come along and change things for the better. The Christian Humanist waits for the rapture while the secular Humanist waits for the utopian products of evolution. Both are historically disappointed because both have placed their hopes in the wrong place.

And then there are the true reformers, revolutionary men and women who understand that we are neither called to escape or evolve, but to seek first His Kingdom in all that we do. Now is the time to change the course of America.

The Presuppositional Mandate: Seek Ye First . . .

The supreme preoccupation of every man should be the Kingdom of God. Like Jesus, the original Kingdom Man, our focus must always be the Father's will. Our focal point of reference should be the establishment of our Father's reign in the earth. The *work* that we are called to do, before we labor for any earthly or material needs, is the work of seeing His righteousness advanced in our world. Though, as I have already pointed out, this idea has fallen in disrepute in our humanistic age, Jesus made this mandate explicitly clear when he said:

> Do not be anxious then, saying, "What shall we eat?" or
> "What shall we drink?" or "With what shall we clothe
> ourselves?" For all these things the Gentiles eagerly
> seek; for your heavenly Father knows that you need all
> these things. But *seek first His Kingdom* and His righ-
> teousness; and all these things shall be added to you.
> (Matt. 6:31-33, emphasis added)

This means that the presuppositional focal point of the
Kingdom Man must be to seek first the Father's will in the
broadest sense. This is not something we do if we have time,
or something we do on Sundays, or something we do at our
Bible studies, or something we do when we "witness." It is our
full-time Kingdom vocation. It is our life. The man who only
seeks to advance God's Kingdom when he has the time has
already left the farm; he is a self-centered Christian. He has not
made the Father's work in the earth his focal orientation. He
has set his vision on something else—himself. This is not biblical Christianity, and it certainly is not Kingdom Manhood.
Rather, it is humanism in religious clothing.

We are called to plug into the Father's work, and since we
are not yet in heaven, the realm we are called to labor in is the
earth. The advancement, then, of the Father's Kingdom, though
it may seem like a spiritual, even ethereal concept, must become the true creed and cry of the King's Man. Coming home
to the Father requires that we turn our attention to the Father's
work. As far as we know, the only prayer Jesus ever taught His
disciples to offer trumpeted the overt petition, "Thy Kingdom
come. Thy will be done, on earth as it is in heaven" (Matt.
6:10). This, too, must become our focal prayer.

Fostering the Inner Revolution

At this point in our progress, one might expect that this
chapter would launch into a discussion on strategy regarding
taking the Kingdom message out to the world. After all, that
is what the world is waiting for, right? Wrong.

What the world is waiting for is to see the visible "witness"
of the Kingdom (Matt. 24:14). Declaration of the Kingdom
gospel is accomplished through our lives more than through
our mouths. This means, in part, that we must embody the

154 ———————————————————————— David E. Long

rule of the Kingdom in such a way that it is demonstrable to the men who are searching for it. As Jesus said, it is our observable "good works" that cause other men to give glory to our Father, not our "good words" (Matt. 5:16). Fostering a biblical revolution, therefore, starts with cultivating an inner change in ourselves.

Like many of the Jews in Jesus' day, most men today think of a modern political concept when they think of a kingdom or a government. But the Kingdom of God is not built the way Satan builds his kingdom. The Kingdom of God is built from the bottom up and the inside out. Whereas the rulers of the world system seek to control people through laws and force, the Kingdom of God starts with the voluntary submission of the individual will (Matt. 7:21). If you do not volunteer, you cannot enter into His Kingdom. So the advancement of our Father's reign starts with constructing the Kingdom of God *in a life*. It starts with me.

Take Responsibility for Your Life

In our day everyone is a victim, and individual "rights" are worshipped. The humanizing of Western culture has produced a generation of individuals who believe they have been victimized by someone's or something's, violating their right to something. Rights advocates now say there is a "right to healthcare" for the sick, a "right to daycare" for the parent, a "right to treatment" for the addict, a "right to housing" for the homeless, a "right to a college education" for everyone, and a "right to sue your parents" for children.[1] Fewer people are willing to take personal responsibility for their own lives and actions while more people are willing to demand their personal "rights."

Not so with the Kingdom Man. Personal responsibility replaces personal rights, and a victorious faith in God's sovereignty replaces the helplessness of victim-minded rationalization. You may have gotten off to a slow start because of poor fathering or worse, but no one can hold you back from becoming a son of God if that is what you set your mind to. Kingdom Manhood is up to you.

Embrace Sonship Today

You can decide today to become a son. Though you will need one or more natural fathers to help you gain experience at it, setting your heart on becoming a son is the first step. Once you have decided that sonship is the relentless goal, the fruit of that decision will come in time. The man who has decided he will become a son will eventually find the father or fathers in the faith he needs to help him. It is true that there are precious few good coaches around, but it is also true that he who seeks finds (Matt. 7:7). Though many will attempt the route of the Macho Man—seeking manhood on their own—the Kingdom Man will embrace the heart of a son and the "ministry" of a father. Even an evil man, like King Saul, can be used to train the man who embraces the call to sonship as tenaciously as David did.

Decide you want to find a "dad." Though this part of your journey will undoubtedly take some time, it must have its genesis. Embrace sonship. I suggest you do it today.

Begin Spending Time with the Heavenly Father

How much time are you spending in the Father's presence every day? Ten minutes? Twenty? The incredible reality is that too many Christian men spend very little time seeking the Father's face on a daily basis.

Are you busy? I can relate. Like most men, my life quickly fills up with everyday affairs. On the vocational level, my days are loaded with seminars and related travel, writing and publishing two newsletters and other writing projects, media and promotional interviews, leaders' meetings, staff meetings, administrative duties, speaking engagements, and more. It is a challenge to squeeze it all into a fifty-five to sixty-hour work week. Then there is the family. On the home front, I face soccer games, piano lessons, dates with my wife and four children, doctors' appointments, meal time, family time, paying the bills, visiting friends and relatives, shopping, attending church, weddings and funerals, fixing the car, and mowing the lawn. Between these two mega-jobs, I have found that I can stay intensely busy from morning 'til night. With everything that is going on in my life, I barely have time left over to sleep, let alone *pray*.

Yet Jesus Himself wandered around in a garden somewhere spending hours in prayer. If God (the Son) needed to pray that much, where do I get off being too important and too busy to spend time with the Father? When the dust settles, the issue is not being too busy. The issue is a poor set of priorities. *Make* time for the Father today, and tomorrow, and the next day. You will not be disappointed.

Establish Kingdom Priorities

Seeking first the Kingdom in my personal life boils down to the idea of setting Kingdom priorities—putting His will first in the use of my limited resources. The least that this means is that I must prioritize spending time with the Father. The man who is unwilling to put God first with his time has not yet made the switch from self-centered Christianity to Father-centered Christianity, or perhaps he is not a Christian at all. His choice of priorities reflects his inner orientation. It is not that we place the football game or our favorite television show as more important than God; it is that we place *ourselves* as more important than God. Otherwise we would shut the thing off.

Establishing Kingdom priorities means overhauling our entire decision-making process. As a Kingdom Man, I must govern my health according to *His* long-term needs for my body, not *my* short-term fleshly desires. Conversely, I must be willing to give up my life and die if necessary to see His righteousness established. Either way my body is to be used for His purposes, not mine. It means I must carefully consider the key relationships I have established relative to whether they advance God's will in and through my life or resist it.[2] It suggests I must seek to maximize my financial holdings and income capabilities so that I can use the growing wealth, not for personal pleasure but to foster that which promotes His will in the world. At the same time, I must be willing to gladly accept the seizure of my property if that is what God wills (Heb. 10:34; Job 1:21).

Our priorities? God first, then family, career, volunteerism, and hobbies. Try it. It works.

Pursue Self-Government

Like many others I typically start off my day in a time of

prayer with the Father. As a framework for my prayer time, I walk through the various segments of the Lord's prayer, the second of which is, "Thy Kingdom come . . ." I have found it helpful to pray this first as an application to my life before applying it to other spheres. Here I ask God, "Is there any area of my life that is not in perfect alignment with your will?" (to which the Spirit usually replies, "Get out a long sheet of paper".)

To bring His reign to the unsubmitted realms of my life, I must learn self-government. This means I must be conscious of the part of me that is in conflict with my spirit. Is this a craving of the flesh, or is this the unfettered longing of the soul? What must I do to make these parts of my being obey the directives of my spirit? Is my spirit even strong enough to walk through this one or do I need the help of a man whose will is sturdier than mine?

Every decision I make must be measured against this question: "Will this personal action advance or retard the righteousness of my Father on the earth?" Fostering the inner revolution takes men who are willing *and* able to rule the inner Kingdom.

Engage Other Men

It may be prudent to recognize and join with a few other men who are also pursuing the Journey to Manhood. Though this is not as essential as finding a father, the mutual encouragement you receive from other men who are headed in the same direction may well be that which keeps you going when the going gets tough. If your church does not provide an environment for men to gather in small groups at least monthly, you may want to simply find two or three other men with whom you could share this book and ask them if they would meet with you weekly or bi-weekly to pray and talk. Use the book as a starting place for discussion. Men's retreats are also good places to help jump-start the process.

Think of Yourself as a Leader

This country would be radically transformed within a generation if every Christian man would begin to think of himself as a leader and pursue becoming fully equipped to faithfully answer that call. Where would mankind be if Christ had denied His leadership calling? In a similar way, where will America be forty years from now if we *accept* ours?

The man who embraces his own call to fatherhood will process life differently than the man who thinks he is only accountable for himself. This kind of man looks at all situations, even apparent failures, as opportunities to learn to lead people better; he is ever in the training mode. If he accepts the biblical leadership paradigm of fatherhood, he will also be sharply attuned to the needs of the people around him.

If a hundred thousand men were to embrace today the call to lead, and were willing to lead as Jesus led, America would be overwhelmed by servanthood in twenty-four hours. Leadership does not begin with authority; leadership begins with service. Authority is gained as a result.

Seek to Be Restored to Your Own Father

At some point in the process, perhaps not now but later, every man should seek to be restored to his own father. The benefits outweigh the risks.

We are an angry people, and more often than not, our anger is rooted in our unwillingness to forgive our dads. This kind of unforgiveness is at the root of our national epidemic of bitterness. Overcoming it is vital in fostering the inner revolution.

It is not our intention here to fully explore the dynamic process of forgiving our fathers; it cannot be dealt with in the space of a few paragraphs. It is, nevertheless, my hope that the father-wounded man will realize his need to set his will to forgive. Though complete forgiveness may take months or even years, it must have a day of conception. There must come a moment in time when a man says, "I will my soul to forgive my dad," though some time may pass before the emotion is completely healed and therefore fully responsive to the will.

In the process of forgiving your father, you may also want to spend some time on his "farm." That is to say, you may want to work with him in some capacity, if this is at all possible. Why? In part, so you can attempt to contribute to his success in some small way. This will foster sonship in your heart and draw out fatherhood in your dad. One man I know drove six hours to spend a few vacation days working with his dad on some apartments his father owned. Another helped his father do some repairs around the house. Still another went to work for his dad in his plumbing business. In working with their dads, even in these small ways, these men *worked* at sonship.

Gordon Dalbey speaks of the vital need for father-son restoration in his book, *Father and Son.*

> The revolutionary work to which God calls men today will not be accomplished by the man who is waiting for the apologies or approval of his father, but only by the one who can accept his father as his own legitimate history. This frees him to begin the painstaking but authentic task of letting the Father God shape him in His image. Such humility opens the man at last to learn the Father's mercy—which restores him to authentic sonship to receive His strength to restore earth as it is in heaven.[3]

In short, fostering the inner revolution begins with my will being daily submitted to the Father's will in the least and the greatest of my decisions. Every determination, whether large or small, must be measured against the criteria of seeking to promote His government first. We will have experienced this dimension of Kingdom Manhood when we can say that which Jesus said as He approached the cruel agony of the cross: "Not my will, but Thine be done" (Luke 22:42).

Fostering the Revolution in the Family

Kingdom men produce Kingdom families. That is to say, they produce men and women who also put first the Father's desires.

Consider the Family Your First Leadership Opportunity

Outside the realm of a man's body, soul, and spirit, the first place in which he should seek to promote the Kingdom of God is in his family. Fostering the bottom-up revolution means leading the members of one's own family toward an intimate relationship with the Father of the universe. This must become one of the most fundamental priorities in a man's life.

A man must ask himself, "Where am I leading my family?" It is not enough that we guide our sons encouragingly through the Mama's Boy, Daddy's Boy, and Man's Man stages of development; we must help them go all the way to the Father. It is not enough that our fathering produces emotionally and physically healthy daughters; we must introduce them to the Father. It is not enough that we love and cherish our wives even as we love ourselves; we must encourage and lead them in finding the Father's heart. We have led the team astray if we have led them elsewhere.

If a son learns to respect his dad because his father treated him with justice and dignity, he will not have trouble respecting his heavenly Father either. If a daughter is nurtured and cared for in her daddy's safe and strong arms, she will not be timid or fearful in the arms of her heavenly Father either. Even a man's wife is more prone to develop an intimate and warm relationship with the Father above if she has enjoyed such a relationship with her husband (and her father) here below.

The sobering leadership challenge comes down to this: Can I successfully guide my family toward the Father? Can I steward these relationships in such a way that I can say to the Father, "I have kept that which You have entrusted to me" (John 17:12)? If I am willing to consider my family the first team for which I am responsible before God, and if I am willing to humbly embrace God's process for training and equipping leaders, then the answer will be yes. On my own I will fail. But with God's help, I will succeed.

Intercede Daily for the Team

Responsibility for people begins in prayer. People belong to the Father, not to us. It is not our job to discover what *we* want them to do; it is our job to discover what *He* wants them to do. Taking each member of the family therefore before the throne daily, agreeing with the Holy Spirit that the Kingdom, or "plan" of God would come to their lives, is the initial act of assuming responsibility for them. Anything else is proud presumption. The man who neglects his familial, high priestly duty before the Father is hard pressed to say that he is leading them for and towards God. He is likely leading them in his own egocentric agenda.

Thy Kingdom come . . . in their lives . . . today. This is the framework for relational intercession. Assuming patriarchal authority in the spirit for our family members against the whiles and schemes of the devil is our first defense relative to "keeping" them in God. Taking our cue from Christ, we need to be able to say that which He said to Peter: "Satan has demanded permission to sift you like wheat; but I have prayed for you" (Luke 22:31, 32). In other words, through Holy Spirit-led prayer we must resist the enemy's power and plan to snatch our family members away from the Father. They are His, but we are the familial shepherd assigned to co-labor with Him in protecting them from the enemy.

In the spirit we must stand daily in the "gates" of this little sheepfold. This is where elders are called to be.

Teach Self-Government

The Kingdom dad and husband fosters the revolution in his family by modeling self-government. If his parental discipline is meted out in anger and lack of control, the children will be hard-pressed to walk in a self-governed way. This means they will never see the Kingdom vividly established in their personal lives because they will have difficulty bringing God's order to the "kingdom of mansoul." But if the father walks in voluntary submission to God and if his own triune nature is in right order, the rest of the team will be predisposed to walk in this way too.

Emphasizing the prospect of ruling the inner kingdom encourages everyone to take responsibility for his actions. The "rights-mania" nonsense is banished as members on the team, from the dad on up, grow daily in their willingness to consciously assume full accountability for their behavior. No one is a victim. The process requires overt training and a ton of modeling. Only as a man walks in inner order and peace himself can he truly begin to train his children to do so.

Think Long-term: Think Grandchildren

Three generations—this is the way God builds something when He is in a hurry. If He is the "God of Abraham, Issac, and Jacob," then I may want to pay attention to His multi-generational strategy.

Like most arrogant Westerners, I often listen to the pompous part of my soul that tells me I can accomplish something significant for God in my lifetime. I can build; I can change; I can do. We plan by the week, or sometimes a few months in advance, and we plan along the lines of what *we* are going to do. The Bible says we should plan our resource strategy for at least the next two generations and that we should think relative to what our *grandchildren* will do (Prov. 13:22). The family vision should be multi-generational.

According to Solomon an unrighteous man is a man who squanders all his means on himself before he dies. The Humanist disinherits his grandchildren because he is only interested in what can be done with his assets while he is alive. His focus is egocentric, and this dictates that he utilize his resources within his own life span on his own projects.

Nevertheless, because the Kingdom Man's focus is Father-centered, he thinks of what could be done over generations. This way of viewing the development of family assets is very liberating because a man sees he can accomplish much more for the Kingdom this way. He is happy to pass on his wisdom, his management skills, his covenant relationships, and his material wealth because he knows that a well-equipped team of, say, fifteen grandchildren could do much more to advance the Father's Kingdom in their day than one moderately equipped person alone. What Israel eventually accomplished in the promised land would have been humanly impossible in Abraham's day. Why? The family was too small.

Put the Family before Career

We have all heard someone say, "You can't take it with you." This is certainly true of a man's career, but it is not true of a man's family. Our covenant relationships will survive the consuming fires of death; our careers will not. For lack of discovering their Kingdom vocation, many men are consumed with the ambitions of their own heart. They are possessed by some earthly pursuit that usually comes in the form of occupational endeavors. Not knowing where they are headed in God's plan, they preoccupy themselves with the distraction of going somewhere in mankind's plan. They are driven to discover in the material world that which they have not been able to discover in the spiritual world; disenchanted, they keep themselves busy.

Conversely, the Kingdom Man knows where he is going in the Father's plan and is unwilling to leave his family behind. His career has become one of many tools he uses to serve God and his family. Carefully stewarding his family for the Father becomes a lifelong goal, one that precedes and supersedes the development of his career.

Serve, Serve, Serve

In summary, the revolution can only be fostered on the family level through servanthood. When we men have become willing to accept the servant-leadership model of Christ, then, and only then, will we enjoy the fruit of ministry He enjoyed. When we can say we have served our family members as Christ served His disciples—with the same level of sacrifice and integrity, the same level of revelation and dedication, the same level of unconditional love—then we can say we have approached the leadership model of Jesus. For Christ did not come to earth to *be* served; He came to earth *to* serve (Matt. 20:28).

So it is with the Kingdom Man—the man who would walk in the revolutionary footsteps of the first Kingdom Man, Jesus Christ.

Fostering the Revolution in the Culture

We have now come to a third level of play—a third arena. The bottom-up revolution that finds its birthplace in the hearts of Kingdom men and in the lives of Kingdom families cannot and should not be contained in these two realms. The revolutionary effects of the Kingdom message are destined to reach the community. It was never God's intention that the blessed fruits of Kingdom order be constrained to the individual or even the Christian family. In fact, the opposite is true. There is a biblical responsibility inherent in the Kingdom message to take the rule of God into every area of culture and society. Jesus said we are the salt of the earth, not the salt of the Church. Anything less than this denigrates our message into a theology of pietistic escapism and results in a cultural leadership vacuum that is eventually filled by pagans of some "ism" variety.

In his book, *The Second American Revolution,* John Whitehead calls for a militancy in fostering the revolution on the cultural level.

> We as Christians must once again commit ourselves to the whole view of Christianity. We must influence all areas of life including law and politics. We can leave nothing untouched by the Bible. We must begin anew to study all intellectual disciplines and apply the Bible to them. We must prepare to be the warriors we should be.[4]

Too many Christian activists think, "If we could just pass this piece of key legislation, or get this particular president elected, everything would be O.K." This explains why so many Christians remained relatively uninvolved in the political or cultural process during the Reagan and Bush presidencies. We were waiting for the home run of the Moral Majority years to have its promised effect. We hit the ball out of the stadium and thought we had won the game.

While home-runs certainly help in the overall strategy of baseball, in the end games are won through scratch singles and by playing all parts of the game well.

Become Versed in a Biblical Worldview

Unbelievably, I was an active Christian in the Church for fifteen years before I ever heard the term "worldview." Not only does the Church, by and large, not teach a biblical worldview, it really does not have one. It has a "heavenview." This is to say, since the heretical doctrines of pietism, along with its secular cousin, humanism, reached the shores of Western Christendom, the Church has lagged way behind in addressing the issues of life on planet earth. We can tell you much about God, heaven, and the future, but geopolitics? education? the arts? environmental care? ethics? the nature of law? national economic design? the role of history?

Without intending to be unkind, we must admit that the majority of Christians and so called Christian leaders in America have little awareness of God's purpose, design, or management philosophy for His world beyond the realm of the local church or Christian family. (Practically speaking, every Christian man would do well to read the book *Understanding the Times*, by David Noebel [see Bibliography], or listen to a tape series on the subject, such as, "Geopolitics, Megatrends and the Christian," by Dennis Peacocke of Strategic Christian Services [see Other Resources].)

Until we recapture an ability to think about life on the planet through a biblical gridwork, a presuppositional framework, we will be lost in terms of fostering the revolution in the culture. We may be well-intentioned reactionaries, but we will undoubtedly lack any serious answers for the crumbling communities and nations we live in.

Get Up to Speed on Current Issues

A biblical worldview is only necessary if one lives and works *in* the world. The man who lives with his family but is never aware of what is going on in the lives of his wife and children cannot claim to be leading them. He may live *with* his family, but he is not living *in* his family.

The same applies to the man who is ignorant of the goings on in society around him. Obviously, the man who is oblivious to current affairs cannot expect to influence them. The man who is unaware of cultural problems cannot lead by offering biblical solutions. Without timely data the Kingdom Man is, at best, like the blind leading the blind. Now is the time for the Christian community of men to open their eyes and get in touch with the issues facing the nation.

How does one stay informed? A careful selection of books, periodicals, newsletters, and newspapers is far better than soaking in the media-speak and overt indoctrination of Peter Jennings and his competing co-conspirators. Further, I can guarantee you will *not* have time to get up to speed on current issues if your evenings are consumed with mindless television entertainment. When pressed for honesty, most men who have told me they were too busy to read were men who were addicted to the talking head in the corner of the living room. Turn the thing off and become a reader.

Prepare for the Long Haul

Fostering the revolution in the community is incredibly difficult with our hurry-up-offense approach. We want to see things get fixed on the cultural level, and we want to see them get fixed now. Never mind that the Humanists have been faithfully working at their cultural agenda for nearly two hundred years, that they moved decisively and strategically over decades with a long-range plan in mind, that they were willing to use a multi-generational strategy (such as, he who controls the kids controls the future [public schools], or he who serves today's family leads tomorrow's family [Planned Parenthood]) to move them closer to their devilish societal goals. Never mind that they were willing to apply Christian-like diligence and patience in seeing their anti-Christian programs legislated and enacted, or that they were willing to pay their dues in the currency of time. We are confident we can turn this situation around in months or, at most, in an election term.

It is time to wake up and admit the obvious—we can't. In fact, shocking as it may sound to many Christians, we are not supposed to. God is unwilling to give His children the land faster than they can steward it. If the political, educational, and business leaders of our nation (just to name three areas) were to announce tomorrow their intention to turn the executive reigns of their respective spheres over to Christians, would we be able to manage them? I am not convinced we could. Certainly, we might bring a fresh moral perspective into these areas, but could we balance the national deficit and eliminate the national debt? Could we produce a national educational agenda and design that which would result in academic excellence for the majority of the students? Could we solve the critical environmental and economic issues facing the business community? In time, probably yes. But in the short run, we might not do any better than the folks running the show right now.

Besides, things generally do not change overnight—they tend to change over generations. The American populace has been immersed in the lawless tenets of humanism for nearly two centuries. History tells us we will not sway an entire nation quickly. Though we may change the heart of the country over a generation (forty years), even that would be a relatively fast work.

As Dr. George Grant so eloquently articulates in his book,

Third Time Around, which chronicles the history of the pro-life movement from the first century to the present, cultural revolution has historically come as a result of the Church's ability to live in the tension between urgency and patience. First he says:

> Clearly there is no room for procrastination or contemplation in times of trouble, distress and calamity. We are called to seize the day. Decisiveness, determination, single-mindedness, constancy, diligence, and passion must inform our agenda. The pace we set should be fervent—because the task before us is urgent.[5]

Two paragraphs later he adds:

> Victory will not be won in a day, however fervently we act. It will take time, perhaps generations. It has always been that way. It always will be.[6]

It could be argued that in recent years the Church has recaptured a sense of urgency in our approach to the culture war. Now it is time to couple this with an intense commitment to persistent patience.

Commit to Strategic Intercession

American Christians will do anything but pray. And generally speaking, men are worse than women.

When a man prays, "Thy Kingdom come, Thy will be done," he must remember the rulers and leaders over him in the world. The Apostle Paul instructed that all Christians must pray for leadership in the community (1 Tim. 2:1-3). It is vital to note that the results of these prayers, according to Paul, would be "tranquility" and the ability to live quiet lives. Peace and tranquillity are the result of the increase of God's government, i.e., His Kingdom (Isa. 9:7).

Praying for our leaders, then, is Kingdom work. In fact, it should be our first Kingdom effort vis-à-vis the community. This should be an integrated dimension of any ongoing gathering of Christian men, whether this is a church men's group, a businessmen's group, a monthly gathering of pastors, or just a few guys who meet occasionally to pray for each other. Men should set the precedent. Kingdom men should pray for the rule of the Father to be advanced on the cultural level.

Discern Your Sphere of Servant Leadership

Every man reading this book is called to leadership on some level. As we have already established, most men are at least called to lead a family. At the most, he is called to leadership in the community.

Jesus sits as the supreme Leader over the entire earth even at this very moment (Eph. 1:20-23). In light of His example, should the Kingdom Man pattern his community involvement otherwise? Should we selfishly pursue a career in our own field of choice while simultaneously shunning Kingdom opportunities to fill leadership posts in the community, whether this be in the business world, politics, the media, education, or any other sphere?

If the civil sphere, for instance, is a "ministry" of God to the people of a given community (Rom. 13:1-4), designed to bring them good, should Kingdom men avoid running for civil office? Should we turn away from God's ministry? More to the point, shouldn't we pursue filling the civil "ministers'" spot with Kingdom men versus those who openly hate God? A Christian man has as much right constitutionally and *more* right spiritually to serve as God's civil "ministers" as anyone.

Jesus said that it was perfectly legitimate to pursue the highest of leadership spots. The catch is we must not seek to lead people the way the "Gentiles," or non-Christians, do. We must *serve* those whom we are called to lead (Matt. 20:25-28). As Dennis Peacocke puts it, "He who serves, leads." This means we must lead as Jesus led; we must be willing to put ourselves at the bottom of the organizational matrix. This turns our humanistic ideas of leadership on their heads.

If we are willing to provide leadership that does not lord itself over the people we are guiding but that supports and serves them with the gifts and resources we have been given, we will see the Kingdom advanced in our communities.

The chart below shows how the righteousness of God is promoted on these three levels—the recipe for a bottom-up revolution.

In the final analysis, we have not embraced the gospel of the Kingdom and true biblical manhood until we have embraced the totality of God's reign in the earth. For truly, "The earth is the LORD's, and all it contains, the world and those who dwell in it (Ps. 24:1)." Our compartmentalized perspective of God's rule has robbed Him of His cosmic sovereignty and erroneously placed Satan as the ruler of the earth. This devilish heresy has done more to neutralize and immobilize the Church and the men of the Church than any frontal attack on the body of Christ ever could have.

It is time to recapture a theology of God's sovereignty in heaven *and* on earth in its fullest context. It is time to export the life and peace of the Kingdom into a culture staggering under the load of death and chaos. It is time to foster a bottom-up change that begins in the hearts of Christian men and reaches every vestige of Western culture. It is time for a revolution.

Fostering the Revolution on Three Levels

Thy Kingdom Come . . .	Key Objective	Vision Banner	Key Strategies
In My Life	The Father's specific will established in my life	The King's Man— One who represents the King to the world	• Daily intercession to seek His will • Development of self-government • Embracing training/authority
In My Family	Father's will established individually and corporately in	The Kingdom Family— The order and peace of God manifest in a small "community"	• Intercession for each member reguarding His will's being established by the family • Teach self-government to members • Provide servant leadership
In My Culture	Father's will established throughout the community and earth	A Christian Community—The tranquility and orderliness of the Kingdom visible in a majority of the people	• Intercession for community leadership regarding His will being established • Provide servant leadership within appointed sphere

Conclusion: A Call to War

In this book I have attempted to uncover the roots of the current cultural crisis in the West. The unfolding nightmare we call modern America is ultimately not the result of corrupt politicians, heretical Keynsian economics, or humanism in the public schools. It is not a result of the ACLU's relentless attack on Christianity, the multi-billion dollar pornography industry, Margaret Sanger's death-on-demand abortion holocaust, the Ivy League's desertion of their Christian heritage, or the propaganda and liberal bias of the media. The New Age, secularism, Liberalism, pluralism, Mormonism, the Jehovah's Witness, feminism, Islam, and every other cultic fad religion are also not at the root of our emerging national disaster.

At the root of the cultural crisis is the curse of the fatherless. The separation of fathers from their children brings upon every culture a cursing of the land like that which we are seeing expressed through the many incredible evils noted above and many more besides. Nevertheless, recognizing this truth is not the same as addressing the problem. Unless the reader is willing to act upon the implications of this message and pursue the Journey to Manhood, this book will have been just another good idea—a meaningless exercise.

Once a man sees what it is he needs to do to get back on course in the journey and then actually steps out to take action, he is guaranteed to meet the resistance of the evil one. At this point the ancient war raging between our Father in heaven and the fallen angel comes crashing into the life of the Kingdom Man.

Therefore, embracing the call to Kingdom Manhood necessitates our embracing the call to war. You cannot have it any other way because the King we all serve is at war. This inevitable confrontation then raises the issue of whether the wounded men of our day will be able to recapture the will to fight. Ultimately, without the restoration of a fighter's will in the hearts of Christian men, there will be no revolution of Kingdom Manhood in this country. Without a dogged determination to attack Satan's deceptive strongholds, there will be no revolution on the level of the family. Without an indefatigable commitment to strike and beat the devil's forces unmercifully, there will be no revolutionary victory in the culture.

The emerging war demands a reawakening of the warrior spirit within the male psyche. In our feminized and pacifistic culture, this is going to be quite a task, but it is possible if we will embrace the biblical call to war that Paul charged his "son" Timothy with nearly two thousand years ago. As you read the following words, remember they were written to a formerly "fatherless" man by the one who had retrained him. As such these words call out to us across the centuries, from one fatherless culture to another, from one dying nation to another, and from one emerging revolution to another. Therefore, in the words of Paul, I challenge you to

> Suffer hardship with me, as a good soldier of Christ Jesus. No soldier in active service entangles himself in the affairs of everyday life, so that he may please the one who enlisted him as a soldier. (2 Tim. 2:3,4)

Are you prepared for what is coming in the days ahead in America? Are you ready for the fallout of God's judgment on this country? Now is the time to put away the comfortable pursuits of civilian life and embrace the call to Kingdom Manhood. Now is the time to get serious about the war that is raging in the heavenlies and to get out onto the playing field—the spiritual battlefield.

I believe we are in a season of grace, and this is permitted by God as a time of preparation for the men of the Kingdom; a time to develop self-government and learn to rule the inner region of "mansoul"; a time to learn to lead; a time to build a strong domestic base and bring our families into Kingdom order; a time to strengthen our resource base; a time to foster a personal relationship with the Father; a time to discover our destiny; a time to experience the security brought about by hearing the Father's voice; a time to test our armor and hone our fighting skills before going to war on the more difficult levels that are sure to come.

Yet, at the same time, I have a sense of urgency. A sense that we should not waste any time, but rather, that we should redeem it for the days are indeed evil (Eph. 5:16). This should motivate us to move forward in fostering the revolution on the first two levels—self-government and family government.

Iron John's dead, but my Father is alive and well, and He is looking for some "real men" who are interested in discovering their destiny in Him. Along with the entire created order, He patiently awaits for the emergence of *all the King's men*.

The revolution begins with you.

Epilogue

Coming to Our Theological Senses

Not everyone who says to me, "Lord, Lord," will enter the Kingdom of heaven; but he who does the will of my Father who is in heaven.

Matthew 7:21

In writing this book, it has been my endeavor to share my heart in a way that was not overtheological or "dry" for the average reader. Though much of what we have been discussing has certainly had theological implications, I have sought to emphasize the practical and applicable. Nevertheless, I think it would be helpful at this point to consciously consider the undergirding theological assumption of this work—the need for the Christian Church to return to a Father-focused Christianity. In essence, the call to Kingdom Manhood is a call to be restored to the Father.

Coming Home to the Father

The central work of Christ's mission on the earth was to open the pathway for you and me to come home to the Father. Like the apostle Paul, every Christian man must bow his knee in the Father's presence (Eph. 3:14) and submit himself to His will. This is the pivotal theme of biblical Christianity. Moreover, it is the defining act of Kingdom Manhood. Consequently, the man who would aspire to genuine Kingdom virility will need to examine his nearness to or distance from this King.

A Wayward Generation of Men

Jesus said to know the Father is to know eternal life (John 17:3); living in separation from the Father is death. This is why Western culture and the men of Western culture are dying— we do not know the Father. Many men, even many Christian men, spend their entire lives distant from their heavenly Father, from the work He has prepared for them, and from the reassuring sound of His voice. This is an unnecessary curse, one I believe will be progressively uprooted as we see a mighty throng of Kingdom Men emerge in America.

Jesus once told a parable of a father and a son. Because of the rich principled truths contained herein, I have chosen this story as a final analogy in seeking to help us to understand our nearness to or distance from the heavenly Father:

> A certain man had two sons; and the younger of them said to his father, "Father, give me the share of the estate that falls to me." And he divided his wealth between them.

> And not many days later, the younger son gathered everything together and went on a journey into a distant country, and there he squandered his estate with loose living. Now when he had spent everything, a severe famine occurred in that country, and he began to be in need.

And he went and attached himself to one of the citizens of that country, and he sent him into his fields to feed the swine. And he was longing to fill his stomach with the pods that the swine were eating, and no one was giving anything to him.

But when he came to his senses, he said, "How many of my father's hired men have more than enough bread, but I am dying here with hunger! I will get up and go to my father, and will say to him, 'Father, I have sinned against heaven, and in your sight; I am no longer worthy to be called your son; make me as one of your hired men.'"

And he got up and came to his father. But while he was still a long way off, his father saw him, and felt compassion for him, and ran and embraced him, and kissed him. And the son said to him, "Father, I have sinned against heaven and in your sight; I am no longer worthy to be called your son." But the father said to his slaves, "Quickly bring out the best robe and put it on him, and put a ring on his hand and sandals on his feet; and bring the fattened calf, kill it, and let us eat and be merry; for this son of mine was dead, and has come to life again; he was lost and has been found." And they began to be merry. (Luke 15:11-24)

Leaving Home

Like the prodigal son, many Christian men in our day have come to believe a lie about the nature of our spiritual inheritance, mentioned by Paul in Ephesians 1. The pivotal issue at stake is this: "Has the Father provided us with the inheritance for our benefit or for His?"

As I have already noted, a theological shift began to occur around the mid-part of the 1800s, where many in the Church began to believe that "salvation" was ultimately a man-centered issue. The thinking became "God sent Jesus to die for *me* so that *I* would not have to suffer in hell." The focus shifted from God to man, from the Father to the children, from the work of the Father's estate to the rewards of Christianity. Subtly and with little fanfare, the philosophy of humanism—the worship of self—began to creep into the Church. This is not a new heresy, of course. The book of Judges chronicles the numerous times the nation of Israel turned from the worship of God to religious practices that centered on their own selfish preferences (Judg. 2:11,12; 4:1; 6:1; 8:33).

When Christianity becomes self-centered, we, in effect, leave the Father's estate. We leave His presence and His will, and we begin to redesign our religious activities to suit ourselves. In short, we learn to worship the god of self.

The "estate" in our story could be compared to our Father's Kingdom—the place where the Father lives, rules, and does His work. It is where Jesus spent His entire adult life and the place where we are called to live and work and eventually find our life because the Father is there. It is the place of life under His reign.

Journey to a Distant Land

When a Christian man (or the entire Christian Church) leaves the Father's estate, he travels to a foreign land of self-serving theology and practice. The focus on the Father's work is replaced with that of his own desires. Though most Christians in our day reject the overt prosperity gospel popularized by a few television evangelists in the 1980s, many have, nevertheless, adopted the basic tenets of this thinking. When our pockets are filled with a rich spiritual inheritance—strong marriages, physical health, mental well-being, peace, and general prosperity of body, soul, and spirit—we often begin to seek to please ourselves. We move from city to city relative to our career pursuits, not necessarily God's. We build bigger homes and purchase whatever luxuries our inheritance can supply, placing less emphasis on tithes and offerings and more on the material pleasures of life. Richly blessed, we sit back and enjoy it.

When we do this, we forget that the inheritance was never meant to be spent selfishly on ourselves; the inheritance was meant to be spent on the work of our Father's estate.

Running Out of Cash

When the prodigal set out to indulge himself on the father's wealth, it did not take very long for his money to disappear.

Had he remained at home and continued to reinvest his share of the family fortune into the ground in the form of seed and sweat, it would have become a replenishing and growing asset. As it was the prodigal chose to consume his inheritance on self-centered living only to discover that when the selfish party, it quickly comes to an end.

Before we can begin to assess our current "resource" situation in the Body of Christ, we must look at what we mean by this term. Resources, in the broadest sense, could include the following:

- revelational resources—what one knows that is useful in accomplishing a task;
- relational resources—those who are assigned to help us in this task;
- communications resources—the means to communicate to others information related to the task;
- administrative resources—the capability to manage the processes involved; and
- material resources—the money, real property, and equipment needed to accomplish the task.[1]

The question then becomes, "Does the Christian Church in America have the broad array of resources needed to play the game of managing God's earth in such a way that His Kingdom is advanced?" The true task, after all, is not managing our own space (i.e., our families or churches); that is the training ground. The true task is managing God's earth. Moreover, at this juncture, the chief manifestation of this task relates primarily to the rebuilding of our towns and cities—from the bottom up.

The prophet Isaiah declared that a people would emerge after the coming of the Messiah who would be characterized as rebuilders of cities. As it relates to the culture, the Church was meant to embrace this ministry:

> Then they will rebuild the ancient ruins, they will raise up the former devastations, and they will repair the ruined cities, the desolations of many generations. (Isa. 61:4)

Let us do a quick inventory then.

The first question is: "Do we have the answers for society, or have we spent our *revelational* resources on ourselves?" Instead of applying biblical principles and strategy to the critical cultural issues of the day in order that His will might be advanced in our communities, we have preoccupied ourselves with more "important" issues, such as figuring out when Jesus will return, or who will be first to be raptured, or whether speaking in tongues is for our time. We have undergone a frontal lobotomy—we have left our brains at the altar. We forgot how to think biblically in the real world.

If we did have the answers, we would not be able to announce them to society because we largely gave away most of our primary communications resources, including the Christian-owned newspapers and, later, the radio and television networks. With the notable exceptions of the Christian Broadcasting Network and the Trinity Broadcasting Network, there are very few Christian organizations seeking to communicate the wisdom of God to the secular masses, let alone to the rulers of our nation. The overwhelming majority of our Christian-owned periodicals, journals, radio stations, and newspapers are designed exclusively for a Christian audience.

We also forfeited the communications resource of statesmanship. When a bill comes before the House and Senate for open floor discussion and a vote, where is the Christian statesman? When the opening of a new Planned Parenthood abortion clinic is debated at the local and state level, where is the Christian statesman? When the local school board is debating the opening of a school-based "health clinic" (meaning "sex clinic"), where is the Christian statesman? When the vital issues of community life are debated and discussed in the community square, wherever that might be, where is the articulate, well-versed Christian statesman? Because the Church has all but disdained involvement in the social order, our young Christian men have shunned this place of strategic service. This was part of our leaving Father's farm in the first place.

If we were to take the time to assess each of the five resource areas relative to the Kingdom task the Father has put before us, we would consistently find a shortage across the board. Because we have not laid up a storehouse of "grain" like Joseph did in Egypt before the days of famine, we will not be in a position to "feed" and lead the people of our nation if a modern-day "famine" hits.

The Inevitability of the Famine

In our story we see that as the prodigal reached the end of his inheritance, he discovered that a famine was coming upon the land. The timing, of course, was very unfortunate. Had the famine struck earlier when the son's pockets were still filled with his father's fortune, he might have fared better than he actually did. On the other hand, had this been the case, he may have never "come to his senses" and headed back home.

In the same way, whenever the Church departs from the Father's estate, theologically speaking, and begins to consume its resources selfishly, it often finds itself running out of "cash" in a terribly inopportune time—a day of famine.

It is interesting to note that the Great Depression of the 1930s arrived concurrent with a time when the Christian Church in our country was experiencing a type of spiritual "bankruptcy." The late Dr. Francis Schaeffer identified the 1930s as a period in which the mainline Protestant churches completed a forty-year shift from orthodoxy to liberalism.[2] The potent and powerful Church of the late 1800s was, in effect, running away from the Father and leaving behind the true work of His estate. Consequently, the Church in the thirties experienced a shortage of resources; it ran out of "cash."

It could be argued that the market crash of 1929 and the resulting economic depression that followed was, at least in part, God's wake up call to the American Church of that period. A case could also be made that though the *institutional* Church may have stayed in the "pig pen," a great number of true believers did, in fact, "come to their senses" and head back toward true, Father-centered Christianity. During the past fifty years, we can see a great "exodus" has occurred as the membership roles of mainline denominations have declined literally by the millions[3] while a significant growth trend has taken place in such churches that have more or less retained an orthodox theological posture.[4] Though it is obvious that some of the defectors have been converting to Mormonism or some other cultic religion, and in this sense, have traded in one "pig pen" for another, it is also obvious that many Christians who were once a part of these prodigal denominations have since made their way back to the Father's estate.

This raises the question of whether or not God might once again use a period of national shortage and distress as His way of revealing the relative insolvency of the prodigal Church and compelling us to move again in the direction of His estate. Is there a "famine" coming? Though many experts are optimistic about the near-term economic outlook for our country, a few are not. A handful of economists from both the Christian and non-Christian sector have come out on the side of gloomy financial forecasts. For instance, in their remarkable work, *The Great Reckoning: How the World Will Change in the Depression of the 1990s,* James Dale Davidson and Lord William Rees-Mogg, two men renown for their uncanny ability to assess megapolitical trends and render accurate forecasts, weigh in with the following assessment:

> One way or the other, we expect a great reckoning. A settling of accounts. We expect the long economic boom and credit expansion that began with World War II to come to an end. The end, when it comes, will not only reveal the insolvency of many individuals and corporations, it may also bring bankruptcy to the welfare state and widespread breakdown of authority within political economies. Such far-reaching transitions cannot occur without touching your life and the lives of those you love. More than you may now imagine, you are vulnerable to financial, economic, and political collapse. You may even be vulnerable to physical violence. The better you can foresee the revolution of the 1990's, the better it will be for you, and not merely in financial terms, but in other ways as well. Your family relationships, your livelihood, the community in which you live will all be altered for better or worse in the great reckoning.[5]

If a national "famine" were to occur, would we have the resources to not only survive, but to actually lead the nation through and out of the crisis? Or would we find ourselves in worse shape than the general population and actually end up in the bondage of the "pig pen?"

Christians in the Pig Pen

Certainly, when Christians become financially indebted to others, they experience a form of slavery. The Bible teaches that debt *is* bondage: "The borrower becomes the lender's slave" (Prov. 22:7). This slavery is easy to see in situations where a man finally wants his wife to quit her job but cannot afford to let her. They are enslaved both to the lenders and their lifestyle. But financial slavery is just one manifestation of the pig pen.

The Bible teaches that when the Church as "salt" refuses to do its job in society, it becomes "good for nothing." When this happens, the Father allows Christians to be "thrown out and trampled under foot by men" (Matt. 5:13). This trampling may be domestic or foreign, meaning God could use our own government or a foreign power to oppress and subjugate the Church. We may see the day in America when Christians have to meet in seclusion for fear of the government, where ministers are licensed by the state and told what they can and cannot say (similar to the current restrictions on a registered 501[c][3] church, only much worse), where Christian parents are imprisoned for spanking their children or for violating a two-child-per-family law, and where public evangelism is seen as treasonous.

I realize this all sounds far-fetched, and Western arrogance tells us it could never happen here. But it has happened before, and it could happen again. The way things are, if it does happen, we will not be able to stop it because we will be *broke*.

Coming Home

As the cyclical pattern in the book of Judges indicates, the prodigal Church usually comes to its senses at some point in the process—typically after the pig pen. The only freedom from the slavery of the pig pen is to return to the Father's estate. The challenge before us as Kingdom Men, then, is to lead the way back to the Father. If we will do that, I believe the rest of society will follow.

Insightfully, Weldon Hardenbrook suggests:

> Men must turn back to knowing God as Father, and the
> Father they must return to is no sweet, feminized, pie-

in-the-sky absentee deity. He is the Patriarch of patri-
archs. He is the ultimate reason that men should be-
have responsibly. There is no hope for the feminized
fathers of America unless they return from the exile of
self-serving and unaccountable behavior and offer their
souls to the mercy of the Father who created them.[6]

Men who embrace the call to Kingdom Manhood must
reach out and seize a defining relationship with the Father. We
must again recapture a theology that includes the Patriarch of
the God-Head. We must seek Him, press into Him, and find
Him. By whatever means, we must make our way home. Moreover, as we come home to the Father, we must come home
with the heart of a servant, humbly putting His agenda and
work before our own. This is the call to the men of the
Kingdom.

Remember the prodigal's father said: "This son of mine
was dead, and has come to life again; he was lost and has been
found." In the same way, Christians are as good as dead to the
Father unless they are preoccupied with the *work* of His Kingdom.

Returning to the estate will not be easy for many. For one
thing, many in the Church have traveled so far from the
Father's presence that it will take a while to get back. They
have a lot of rethinking to do. Someone will have to help them
find their way. For others, the paradigm shift from self-centered Christianity to Father-centered Christianity will be so
emotionally strenuous that they will resist "coming to their
senses." It is possible, I suppose, that some men may never
come home, preferring to live out their lives in the slavery of
the pig pen.

Even so, many will return to the Father and to the work of
His estate and will be happy to do so. When this happens a
final lesson of the prodigal will be experienced in the Church.

Recapturing the Joy of Working for the Father

Work is not a curse; it is our life. A man has not truly lived
until he has experienced the work he was created to accomplish. Anything less is just hanging out—hanging out for Jesus,
for retirement, or to die.

Many men in our country, including many men in the Church, consider *work* a part of the curse that resulted from Adam's fall. We see it as a necessary evil, something we must do to get by. Like the Humanist we look forward to retiring from it when we turn sixty-five. Yet, on closer examination, we see that the work-mandate and work itself actually preceded the Fall in that Adam was commanded to cultivate and keep the garden. He was the first worker, and God was his boss. This type of arrangement is the way work was meant to be.

It is high time Christian men, in coming to their senses, reject the humanistic notion that work is a four-lettered word, an onerous expenditure of time to be avoided at all cost. For at the center of the message of biblical Christianity is the idea that we are called to labor for and with our heavenly Father, for the advancement of His will. When we find this labor, we will find that doing the work we were created to do is anything but burdensome (Matt. 11:29, 30).

Like Jesus (the second Adam), the first Adam used to walk with God in the cool of the evening. Though the Bible does not exactly say so, I suspect they were discussing Adam's work. After all, how was Adam to know what to do or how to do it? There were no universities where he could study agriculture, and he could not ask his neighbor because he did not have one. I believe the Father personally gave him his instructions in these walks, just as He later did with Christ each morning and evening.

If work is a curse, then the Father and Christ are both under it because Jesus said that His Father was still working and so He must work (John 5:17). Obviously, this is preposterous, yet many in our day view work through this faulty paradigm. Jesus found His life and calling in the work He did with His Father. In fact, Christ's work was the basis of His fellowship with the Father. So it is with us.

When the Industrial Revolution separated sons from their fathers, it also separated sons from their fathers' work, inevitably giving way to the notion that work itself was evil.[7] This notion was carried over into our spiritual lives, and we began to view Christianity as getting "saved" instead of as an opportunity to be rejoined to our Father's work. Though the Bible clearly teaches that we are not saved *by* work, it does teach that we are saved *to* work (Eph. 2:10; 4:12). We are rescued from death so as to enter into the work of our heavenly Father.

When the prodigal returned to his father, he returned to his father's work as well. He went home to serve, and in doing so he found his life. When the son was gone from the estate, his father considered him as good as dead. The son, in fact, came home with the idea in mind that if he did not return to the work of his father's estate he might actually die. He discovered that working for others was a curse, but working for Dad was a blessing.

Developing this Father-focused work orientation is critical, because until we are willing to work for our heavenly Father, not just know Him, we are truly dead to Him. What would Christ's life have looked like had he not connected with His Father's work? His very existence sprang from His relationship with His Father. He said He could only do the work that the Father told Him to (John 5:19). When He finished the job He was sent to do, He gave up His life and died.

King David, another Kingdom Man, also preoccupied himself with the Father's work. The Bible tells us that he completely fulfilled the purpose of God in his generation; then he went to sleep (Acts 13:36). This is the way it should be with us.

A man finds joy in working for the Father. This is the simple message of the gospel that Jesus preached. Until a man finds and does that work, he will spend his life searching for something meaningful to do here below.

Conclusion: Kingdom Men Must Recapture a Father-centered View of Reality

A theological perspective of the situation in which we find ourselves is absolutely critical. First in the Church, and then in the culture at large, every society must come to the place where it recognizes *Who* God is. Otherwise it will perish.

As men we must each come to the place where we admit that there is an innate sense in us that we were born with the need to have purpose in our lives. That purpose is only found on our Father's estate—the place of our Father's presence and work. All other pursuits lead us to the pig pen, and unless we come to our senses, these pursuits will eventually lead us to death. Far too many men in America today, including many Christian men, exist in this aimless and impoverished state.

All that I have shared in the pages of this book will ultimately bear little fruit in a man's life unless he has made a conscious decision to make the Father the centerpiece of His theology and worldview and seek the Father as his closest spiritual relationship. Otherwise, regardless of how many books a man reads, he will continue to live in a state of "deadness" to the Father. As far as the Father is concerned, the son who has not yet come home has not yet come back to life.

Moreover, anything less than a Father-centered view of Christianity will continue to produce deadness in the wider Body of Christ, resulting in deadness in the culture. The self-focused man seeks to draw near to the Father for his own selfish gain; he arrives at the Father's doorstep to get the "goods" of Christianity. Then he leaves the estate. Then he dies. And America dies with him.

Though we as Christian men may be far from the high ideals of Kingdom Manhood at this point, it is, nevertheless, my conviction and my prayer that a revival of royal masculinity is about to take place in our day. Ideas do have their consequences, and the idea of recapturing a Father-centered view of reality will likely have the consequence of producing a revived sense of Kingdom destiny in the men of our day.

If you are a man seeking for truth, I invite you to accept Christ's invitation to come to your theological senses and come home to the Father.

May you find the King. Amen.

Notes

Introduction

[1]*Respectfully Quoted: A Dictionary of Quotations From the Congressional Research Service*, Suzy Platt, editor, Congressional Research Division, Washington, D.C., Library of Congress, 1989, 84 (citation #424)

Chapter One

[1]William H. Masters, Virginia E. Johnson, and Robert C. Kolodny, *Human Sexuality Third Edition* (Glenview, IL: Scott Foresman & Company, 1988), 403.

[2]N. M. Malmuth, M. Heim, and S. Fescbach, *Journal of Personality and Social Psychology* 38 (1980): 399-408.

[3]*Information Please Almanac, Atlas & Yearbook 1993*, 46th edition, Otto Johnson, ed. (Boston, MA: Houghton Mifflin Company, 1992), 472.

[4]Ibid., 470.

[5]George Barna, *America 2000: What the Trends Mean for Christianity* (Glendale, CA: The Barna Research Group, 1989), 20.

[6]Masters, *Human Sexuality*, 261.

[7]Diana M. Elliott, Ph.D., and John Briere, Ph.D., "The Sexually Abused Boy: Problems in Manhood," *Medical Aspects of Human Sexuality* (February 1992): 1.

[8]*Information Please*, 472.

[9]*Statistical Abstract of the United States*, U.S. Bureau of the Census, 1992, Washington, DC, 457.

[10]*Information Please*, 471.

[11]*Statistical Abstract of the United States 1990*, U.S. Bureau of the Census, 1990, Washington, DC, 45.

[12]*Statistical Abstract of the United States 1992*, U.S. Bureau of the Census, 1990, Washington, DC, 457.

[13]Francis Schaeffer, *The Great Evangelical Disaster* (Westchester, IL: Crossway Books, 1984), 37.

[14]Edwin Lewis Cole, *On Becoming a Real Man* (Nashville: Thomas Nelson Publishers, 1992), 3.

[15]Ibid.

[16]Karen S. Peterson, "New Rules Make Men Underdog in Game of Love," *USA Today* (31 July 1992): 5D.

[17]Nancy Gibbs, "Man and Woman," *Time* 139 (6 January 1992): 47.

[18]"Next, the 'Bottom-Free 7'?," *Democrat & Chronicle* (12 July 1992): 10A; and Carol Ritter, "Artistic Dancers go Topless," *Democrat & Chronicle* (10 July 1992): 1B.

[19]John Piper and Wayne Grudem, *Recovering Biblical Manhood and Womanhood: A Response to Evangelical Feminism* (Wheaton IL: Crossway Books), 34.

Chapter Two

[1]Don Feder, "Fatherless families may be greatest challenge of present generation," *AFA Journal* (March 1992): 20.

[2]William J. Bennet, *Our Children and our Country* (New York: Simon and Schuster, 1988), 64.

[3]Barbara Dafoe Whitehead, "Dan Qualye Was Right," *The Atlantic Monthly* (April 1993): 71.

[4]Weldon M. Hardenbrook, *Missing From Action* (Nashville: Thomas Nelson, Inc., 1987), 51.

[5]Ibid., 52.

[6]Robert Bly, *Iron John* (New York: Addison-Wesley Publishing Company, Inc., 1990), x.

[7]*Marital Status and Living Arrangements: March 1992*, U.S. Bureau of the Census, Current Population Reports, Series P20, No.468, Washington, DC, 1992, XIII.

[8]Michael E. Lamb, ed., *The Role of the Father in Child Development* (New York: John Wiley and Sons, 1976), 21.

[9]Steven Farmer, *The Wounded Male* (New York: Ballantine Books, 1991), 24.

[10]Dr. James Dobson and Gary L. Bauer, *Children at Risk* (Dallas, TX: Word Publishing, 1990), 167.

[11]Feder, "Fatherless families," 20.

[12]Lamb, *The Role of the Father*, 18.

[13]Ibid.

[14]Ibid., 234.

[15]Dobson and Bauer, *Children at Risk*, 167.

[16]Ibid., 167-168.

[17]Ibid., 170.

[18]Steven Mills, "Physician won't be intimidated on abortion," *Democrat & Chronicle* (5 July 1992): 1A (quoting Rochester-area abortionist Morris Wortman).

[19]Randall A. Terry, *Accessory to Murder* (Brentwood, TN: Wolgemuth & Hyatt Publishers, Inc., 1990), 47.

[20]Whitehead, "Dan Quayle," 77.

[21]Ibid., 80.

[22]Feder, "Fatherless families," 20.

[23]Hardenbrook, *Missing From Action*, 73-74.

[24]Bly, *Iron John*, 23.

Chapter Three

[1]Erik H. Erikson, *Childhood and Society*, 2d ed. (New York: W. W. Norton and Company, 1963), 249.

[2]Alexander Mitscherlich, *Society without the Father: A Contribution to Social Psychology* (New York: Harcourt, Brace & World, Inc., 1969 [English copyright]), 60.

³Ibid., 134.

⁴W. Peter Blitchington, *Sex Roles and the Christian Family* (Wheaton, IL: Tyndale House Publishers, Inc., 1980), 111.

⁵Stanton L. Jones, *The Crisis of Homosexuality,* J. Isamu Yamamoto, ed. (Wheaton, IL: Victor Books, 1990), 109.

⁶Blitchington, *Sex Roles,* 141.

⁷Hardenbrook, *Missing From Action,* 16.

⁸Robert Bly, *Iron John* (New York: Addison-Wesley Publishing Company, Inc., 1990), 106.

Chapter Four

¹Dr. Frank Minirth, Dr. Brian Newman, and Dr. Paul Warren, *The Father Book: An Instruction Manual* (Nashville: Thomas Nelson, Inc., 1992), 64-65.

²Gordon Dalbey, *Father & Son: The Wound, The Healing, The Call to Manhood* (Nashville: Thomas Nelson, Inc., 1992), 36.

³Ibid., 40.

Chapter Five

¹Ted W. Engstrom, *The Fine Art of Mentoring: Passing On to Others What God Has Given to You* (Brentwood, TN: Wolgemuth & Hyatt, Publishers, Inc. 1989), 4-5.

Chapter Six

¹"Legalizing Adultery," *Freedoms Alert* (June 1993): 2.

²Charlotte M. Mason, *Home Education, "Training and educating children under nine,"* The Original Home Schooling Series, Vol. 1, (Wheaton, IL: Tyndale House Publishers, Inc., 1989), 317.

³Ibid., 317-318.

Chapter Seven

¹Ray Sutton, in his scholarly work, *That You May Prosper: Dominion By Covenant* (Tyler, TX: Institute for Christian Economics, 1987), puts forth this idea—that the biblical covenant is built around a five-point structure that mirrors the ancient king-vassal treaties—and does so with convincing authority. I recommend his book to the serious student of the gospel of the Kingdom.

²Weldon M. Hardenbrook, *Missing From Action* (Nashville: Thomas Nelson, Inc., 1987), 73-76.

³Robert Bly, *Iron John* (New York: Addison-Wesley Publishing Company, Inc., 1990), 106.

⁴Francis Schaeffer, *The Great Evangelical Disaster* (Westchester, IL: Crossway Books, 1984), 183.

⁵Doug LeBlanc, "Ideas have consequences: Educators criticize evangelical 'pressure groups,'" *World* (22 May 1993): 13.

⁶Ibid.

⁷Schaeffer, 34.

⁸John W. Whitehead, *The Second American Revolution* (Westchester, IL: Crossway Books, 1988), 39-40.

⁹Paul Kurtz, ed., *Humanist Manifesto I* (Buffalo, NY: Prometheus Books, 1984), 10.

Chapter Eight

¹*Webster's New World Dictionary of American English,* 3d college ed., Victoria Neufeldt, ed. (New York, NY: Webster's New World Dictionaries), 767.

²Gary Smalley and John Trent, Ph.D., *The Blessing* (Nashville: Thomas Nelson Publishers, 1986), 24.

³Weldon Hardenbrook in *Recovering Biblical Manhood and Womanhood,* John Piper and Wayne Grudem, eds., (Wheaton, IL: Crossway Books, 1991), 378.

⁴Don Eberly, "Finding Common Ground With our Neighbors," *Focus on the Family Citizen* (21 December 1992): 15.

⁵Ibid.

⁶Tom Marshall, *Understanding Leadership: Fresh Perspectives on the Essentials of New Testament Leadership* (Chischester, England: Sovereign World Ltd., 1991), 11.

⁷Ibid.

⁸Dennis Peacocke, *Winning the Battle for the Minds of Men* (Santa Rosa, CA: Alive & Free, 1987), 108.

⁹The term "pagan" is not meant here to be derogatory. Rather, "pagan" is the biblical term for "non-believer" (Ez. 10:2; Neh. 13:26; Hos. 5:7; Zeph. 1:4). I use the term for biblical accuracy and to

dramatize the idea that those who reject Christ's lordship and teachings, those who are outside of His covenant, are the ones currently ruling *His* earth and stewarding *His* wealth (in regards to joint community resources). Biblically we understand that the political arena is a ministry of God to the citizens of a community (Rom. 12) and therefore cannot be considered a secular realm outside of God's plan for Christians to lead. Obviously those who reject His Lordship, the pagans, are not going to lead the political process relative to biblical ethics, which accounts for the moral chaos we see in most communities.

[10]Peacocke, *Winning the Battle*, 109.

[11]Marshall, *Understanding Leadership*, 11.

Chapter Nine

[1]John Leo, "The spread of rights babble," *U.S. News & World Report* (28 June 1993): 17.

[2]The idea of prioritizing relationships merits further elaboration. Jesus said," *"Do not think that I came to bring peace on earth; I did not come to bring peace, but a sword. For I came to set a man against his father, and a daughter against her mother, and a daughter-in-law against her mother-in-law; and a man's enemies will be the members of his household. He who loves father or mother more than Me is not worthy of Me; and he who loves son or daughter more than Me is not worthy of Me"* (Matt. 10:34-37).

In Western humanistic culture, we have come to regard the individual with higher significance than God. Consequently, when confronted with the idea that a father or mother or a son or daughter could actually be detrimental to seeing God's will established in a person's life, we sometimes put the relative or relationship first and God's will second. To keep "peace" in the family, we give up true peace with God. Though it may in certain situations seem cruel or unkind to the human-focused way of our thinking, we must always place God's will as a higher priority than our own, even if in doing so it means we disappoint or anger a close friend or relative. This is perhaps one of the hardest ideas for American Christians to contemplate because of our human-focused worldview, but placing people or people's feelings before obeying God is a pagan, not Christian idea.

It must be strenuously called out that we can never use this as a rationale for deliberately hurting others or for acting self-willed or self-centered in the name of God. Saying, "God told me to . . ." as an indisputable rationale for doing our own thing is a heinous and rebellious act. Though we see many abusing this idea in this way, it, nevertheless, does not negate the biblical nature of the principle of putting God's Kingdom before the feelings or preferences of others.

[3]Gordon Dalbey, *Father & Son: The Wound, The Healing, The Call to Manhood* (Nashville: Thomas Nelson, Inc., 1992), 180.

[4]John W. Whitehead, *The Second American Revolution* (Westchester, IL: Crossway Books, 1988) , 159.

[5]Dr. George Grant, *Third Time Around: The History of the Pro-Life Movement from the First Century to the Present* (Brentwood, TN: Wolgemuth & Hyatt, 1991), 171.

[6]Ibid., 172.

Epilogue

[1]For further study on these five areas of resources, I would suggest the leadership tape series, *Strategic Thinking*, by Dennis Peacocke, Strategic Christian Services, 1221 Farmer's Lane, Suite B, Santa Rosa, CA, 95405.

[2]Francis Schaeffer, *The Great Evangelical Disaster* (Westchester, IL: Crossway Books, 1984), 32-37.

[3]George Barna, *The Church Today: Insightful Statistics and Commentary* (Glendale, CA: The Barna Research Group, 1990), 24-26.

[4]Dean M. Kelly, *Why Conservative Churches Are Growing* (Macon, GA: Mercer University Press, 1984), 1-16, 26.

[5]James Dale Davidson and Lord William Rees-Mogg, *The Great Reckoning: How the World Will Change in the Depression of the 1990s* (New York: Summit Books, 1991), 12-13.

[6]Weldon H. Hardenbrook, *Missing From Action* (Nashville: Thomas Nelson, Inc., 1987) , 141.

[7]Alexander Mitscherlich, *Society Without the Father* (New York: Tavistock Publications Limited, 1969), 150-164. Mitscherlich's work, though mixed with much Freudian philosophy, nevertheless brings out the debilitating effects of fatherlessness on many levels from a psycho-analytical perspective. In relationship to the issue of work, he observes that the son grows suspicious of the father when he cannot see him work. The son might think, "Dad must be evil, else he would not try to hide what he is doing from me. Besides, if he was 'good,' he would stay home with me." This suspicion, Mitscherlich holds, leads to a corresponding suspicion of "work" itself.

Bibliography

On manhood and family:

Becker, Verne. *The Real Man Inside: How Men Can Recover Their Identity and Why Women Can't Help*. Grand Rapids, MI: Zondervan Publishing House, 1992.

Blitchington, Peter W. *Sex Roles & the Christian Family*. Wheaton, IL: Tyndale House Publishers, Inc., 1984.

Bly, Robert. *Iron John: A Book About Men*. New York: Addison-Wesley Publishing Company, Inc., 1990.

Canfield, Ken R. *The 7 Secrets of Effective Fathering*. Wheaton IL: Tyndale House Publishers, Inc., 1992.

Clark, Stephen B. *Man and Woman in Christ: An Examination of the Roles of Men and Women in the Light of Scripture and the Social Sciences*. Ann Arbor, MI: Servant Books, 1980.

Cole, Edwin Louis. *Maximized Manhood: A Guide to Family Survival*. Springdale, PA: Whitaker House, 1982.

Cole, Edwin Louis. *On Becoming a Real Man*. Nashville: Thomas Nelson Publishers, 1992.

Conway, Jim. *Men in Mid life Crisis*. Elgin, IL: David C. Cook Publishing Co., 1981.

Dalbey, Gordon. *Father and Son: The Wound, the Healing, the Call to Manhood*. Nashville: Thomas Nelson Publishers, 1992.

Dalbey, Gordon. *Healing The Masculine Soul: An Affirming Message for Men and the Women Who Love Them*. Dallas: Word Publishing, 1988.

Dobson, Dr. James C. *Straight Talk to Men and Their Wives*. Waco, TX: Word Books, 1980.

Engstrom, Ted W. *The Fine Art of Mentoring: Passing On to Others What God Has Given to You*. Brentwood, TN: Wolgemuth & Hyatt, Publishers, Inc., 1989.

Erikson, Erik H. *Childhood and Society*. New York: W.W. Norton & Company Inc., 1950.

Farmer, Steven. *The Wounded Male*. New York: Ballantine Books, 1991.

Farrar, Steve. *Point Man: How a Man Can Lead a Family*. Portland, OR: Multnomah Press, 1990.

Gilder, George. *Men and Marriage*. Gretna, LA: Pelican Publishing Company, 1986.

Gilmore, David D. *Manhood in the Making: Cultural Concepts of Masculinity*. New Haven: Yale University Press, 1990.

Hardenbrook, Weldon M. *Missing From Action*. Nashville: Thomas Nelson Publishers, 1987.

Hicks, Robert. *Uneasy Manhood: The Quest for Self-Understanding*. Nashville: Oliver Nelson (a division of Thomas Nelson), 1991.

Keen, Sam. *Fire in the Belly: On Being a Man*. New York: Bantam Books, 1991.

Lamb, Michael E., ed. *The Role of the Father in Child Development*. New York: A Wiley Interscience Publication, 1976.

Minirth, Dr. Frank, Dr. Brian Newman and Dr. Paul Warren. *The Father Book: An Instruction Manual*. Nashville: Thomas Nelson Publishers, 1992.

Mitscherlich, Alexander. *Society Without the Father: A Contribution to Social Psychology*. New York: Harcourt, Brace & World, Inc., 1963.

Morley, Patrick M. *The Man in the Mirror: Solving the 24 Problems Men Face*. Brentwood, TN: Wolgemuth & Hyatt Publishers, Inc., 1989.

Piper, John, and Wayne Grudem. *Recovering Biblical Manhood and Womanhood: A Response to Evangelical Feminism.* Wheaton, IL: Crossway Books (a division of Good News Publishers), 1991.

Smalley, Gary, and John Trent. *The Blessing.* Nashville: Thomas Nelson Publishers, 1986.

Stoop, David. *Making Peace With Your Father.* Wheaton, IL: Tyndale House Publishers, Inc., 1992.

Yamamoto, Isamu J., ed. *The Crisis Of Homosexuality.* Wheaton IL: Victor Books (a division of Scripture Press Publications Inc.), 1990.

On the Church in society:

Aburdene, Patricia, and John Naisbitt. *Megatrends for Women.* New York: Villard Books, 1992.

Antonio, Gene. *Aids: Rage & Reality: Why Silence is Deadly.* Dallas: Anchor Books, 1993.

Barna, George. *The Barna Report 1992-93: America Renews its Search for God.* Ventura, CA: Regal Books, 1992.

Blamires, Harry. *Recovering the Christian Mind: Meeting the Challenge of Secularism.* Downers Grove, IL: InterVarsity Press, 1988.

Chilton, David. *Paradise Restored: A Biblical Theology of Dominion.* Ft. Worth, TX: Dominion Press, 1987.

Dawson, John. *Taking Our Cities For God: How to Break the Spiritual Strongholds.* Lake Mary, FL: Creation House, 1989.

DeMar, Gary, and Peter J. Leithart. *The Reduction of Christianity: Dave Hunt's Theology of Cultural Surrender.* Ft. Worth, TX: Dominion Press, 1988.

DeMar, Gary. *Ruler of the Nations: Biblical Principles for Government.* Ft. Worth, TX: Dominion Press, 1987.

Dobson, Dr. James, and Gary L. Bauer. *Children at Risk: The Battle for the Hearts and Minds of Our Kids.* Dallas: Word Publishing, 1990.

Dugan, Jr., Robert P. *Winning the New Civil War: Recapturing America's Values.* Portland, OR: Multnomah, 1991.

Evans, Anthony T. *America's Only Hope: Impacting Society in the '90s.* Chicago: Moody Press, 1990.

Frangipane, Francis. *The Three Battlegrounds.* Marion, IA: n.p., 1989.

Glessner, Thomas A. *Achieving an Abortion-Free America by 2001*. Portland, OR: Multnomah, 1990.

Grant, Dr. George. *Third Time Around: A History of the Pro-Life Movement from the First Century to the Present*. Brentwood, TN: Wolgemuth & Hyatt, Publishers, Inc., 1991.

Medved, Michael. *Hollywood vs. America: Popular Culture and the War on Traditional Values*. New York: Harper Collins Publishers, 1992.

Naisbitt, John, and Patricia Aburdene. *Megatrends 2000: Ten New Directions for the 1990's*. New York: Avon Books, 1990.

Noebel, David A. *Understanding the Times: The Story of the Biblical Christian, Marxist/Leninist, and Secular Humanist Worldviews*. Manitou Springs, CO: Summit Press, 1991.

North, Gary. *Unholy Spirits: Occultism in the New Age*. Ft. Worth, TX: Dominion Press, 1988.

Peacocke, Dennis. *Winning the Battle for the Minds of Men*. Santa Rosa, CA: Alive & Free, 1987.

Reagan, Ronald. *Abortion and the Conscience of the Nation*. Nashville: Thomas Nelson Publishers, 1984.

Rushdoony, Rousas J. *The Institutes of Biblical Law*. The Presbyterian and Reformed Publishing Company, 1973.

Schaeffer, Francis A. *The Great Evangelical Disaster*. Westchester, IL: Crossway Books (a division of Good News Publishers), 1984.

Schaeffer, Franky. *Bad News for Modern Man: An Agenda for Christian Activism*. Westchester, IL: Crossway Books (a division of Good News Publishers), 1984.

Terry, Randall A. *Accessory to Murder: The Enemies, Allies, and Accomplices to the Death of our Culture*. Brentwood, TN: Wolgemuth & Hyatt, Publishers, Inc., 1990.

Terry, Randall A. *Operation Rescue*. Springdale, PA: Whitaker House, 1988.

Whitehead, John W. *The Second American Revolution*. Westchester, IL: Crossway Books (a division of Good New Publishers), 1982.

On leadership:

Butt, Howard. *The Velvet Covered Brick: Christian Leadership in an Age of Rebellion*. New York: Harper and Row, Publishers, 1973.

DePree, Max. *Leadership Is an Art*. New York: Dell Publishing, 1989.

Joyner, Rick. *Leadership, Management and the Five Essentials for Success*. Pineville, NC: Morning Star Publications, 1990.

Marshall, Tom. *Understanding Leadership: Fresh Perspectives on the Essentials of New Testament Leadership*. Chichester, England: Sovereign World, 1991.

Roberts, Wess. *Leadership Secrets of Attila the Hun*. New York: Warner Books, 1985.

Smith, Fred. *Learning to Lead: Bringing Out the Best in People*. Waco, TX: Word Books Publisher, 1986.

On the possibility of a coming "famine":
Davidson, James Dale, and Lord William Rees-Mogg. *The Great Reckoning: How the World Will Change in the Depression of the 1990s*. New York: Summit Books, 1991.

Burkett, Larry. *The Coming Economic Earthquake*. Chicago: Moody Press, 1991.

Figgie, Jr., Harry E., with Gerald J. Swanson. *Bankruptcy 1995: The Coming Collapse of America and How to Stop It*. Boston: Little, Brown and Company, 1992.

Other Resources

Christian Service Brigade
Box 150
Wheaton, IL 60187
(708) 665-0630
  • Newsletter: *On the Father Front* and *Man to Man*

Dad the Family Shepherd
Dave Simmons
P.O. Box 21445
Little Rock, AR 72221
(501) 221-1102; 1 (800) 234-3237
  • Seminars (live, audio, and video), men's ministries, small group materials, books, newsletters

Focus on the Family
Colorado Springs, CO 80995
(719) 633-6287; 1 (800) 232-6459
  • Videos, films: *A Father Looks Back* and *Christian Fathering*
  • Newsletter: *Parental Guidance* (for parents of teens)

National Center for Fathering
217 Southwind Place
Manhattan, KS 66502
(913) 776-4114
  • Personal Fathering Profile, research

Promise Keepers
P.O. Box 18376
Boulder, CO 80308
(303) 421-2800
  • Leadership and men's conferences

Strategic Christian Services
1221 Farmer's Lane, Suite B
Santa Rosa, CA 95405
  • Newsletter: *The Rebuilders* (ministry to cities) and the *Bottom Line* (cultural commentary)
  • Leadership seminars, national leadership institute, national youth interns program

God's World, Publications, Inc.
Box 2330
Asheville, NC 28802
1 (800) 951-6397
- Weekly news periodical with a biblical perspective

About the Author

David Long has been involved in challenging and equipping Christians to impact the culture since 1985 when he founded the pro-life group, Project Life of Rochester. The following year, he founded The Problem Pregnancy Centers and assisted in the formation of the Open Home Ministry, both outreaches to pregnant women.

As director of Project Life, David was arrested thirteen times in five different cities for pro-life activism and was jailed on three occasions, spending a total of sixty-seven days in jail. He has led numerous pro-life demonstrations and pro-life rescue missions in the Rochester, New York, area and assisted Operation Rescue National in regional rescue campaigns in New York and Philadelphia.

In 1989, David founded *Christians In Action*, a leadership development agency designed to assist the local church in equipping the Saints to impact the culture. As a motivational speaker and seminar instructor, David seeks to train and mobilize Christians to impact the culture through servant leadership. In this vein, David is a co-founder of the Rochester Area Metro Action council, a servant-leadership effort of area business leaders, pastors, and applied ministry leaders.

Through *Christians In Action*, David is involved in serving Christian leaders in several cities in the development of regional strategy for advancing God's righteousness and for mobilizing the Christian community. He is also a frequent speaker at men's retreats and other gatherings of men.

David resides in Wolcott, New York, with his wife Diana and their four children.

About:
Christians In Action
Ministries, Inc.

Christians In Action is a Christian organization dedicated to assisting the local church in equipping the Saints for culture-changing works of service. Our services are as follows:

- Newsletters:

  Off The Wall: The Publication for All The King's Men— Published monthly, this newsletter seeks to encourage and strengthen the emerging army of Kingdom Men through biblical teaching and testimony. **Available spring 1994**—subscription rate: $18 per year. Write for a courtesy three-month subscription.

  Culture Changers: The Publication for Christians In Action— News and views from a biblical perspective. Published monthly (except August). Suggested donation $20 per year.

- Seminars (live and audio):

  All The King's Men—Challenging and equipping men to aspire to Kingdom Manhood

  The *Christians In Action* Seminar—Basic training for local churches seeking to engage and change the community

  The Pro-life Mobilization Seminar—Development of church-based pro-life action ministry

- *Christians In Action* affiliate development program:

  Regional leadership and strategy development for impacting community and mobilizing the Christian Church

- Annual leadership and men's conferences

For more information, write
Christians In Action Ministries, Inc.
P.O. Box 98
Wolcott, NY 14590-0098

Order A Complimentary
Three-Month Subscription To:

Off The Wall: The Publication for All The King's Men

At the time of this printing, our staff is in the process of development for a new newsletter for men entitled *Off The Wall*. We anticipate a spring 1994 launch date. If you would like to order a complimentary three-month subscription to this monthly newsletter, simply use the coupon below. We will also keep you informed of other available materials for men and related men's events in your area.

- -

Dear David,

_____ Please send me a free three-month trial subscription, *Off The Wall*.

_____ Please keep me informed of other available materials for men and of related men's events in my area.

_____

name

_____

address

_____

city, state, zip

Mail to:
Christians In Action Ministries, Inc.
P.O. Box 98,
Wolcott, NY 14590-0098